W9-CSD-231

Pelican Books
The Making of Feature Films – A Guide

Ivan Butler was born in Heswall, Cheshire. He was educated
at St Edward's School, Oxford, and from there went to the
Central School of Speech Training and Dramatic Art. He
has spent many years in the professional theatre, as actor,
writer and producer. Over twenty of his plays have been
staged, and he has also written for radio and television, in
addition to numerous articles on theatrical subjects and
a handbook on producing pantomime and revue.

Since the nineteen-twenties he has been a keen film
enthusiast. His writings in this field include books on the
horror film and on religion in the cinema, and articles on
the history and development of cinema buildings in
England, on the Children's Film Foundation, and (in
preparation) Shakespeare on the screen. His most recent
book is a study of the films of Roman Polanski, and he is
at present writing the authorized history of the British Film
Institute. He is on the lecture panel of the British Film
Institute, and has conducted a number of weekend courses
on the cinema.

Ivan Butler is married, with one son, and lives in
Northwood, Middlesex.

Ivan
Butler

The Making of Feature Films

A Guide

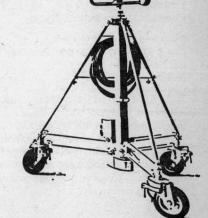

Penguin Books

Penguin Books Ltd, Harmondsworth,
Middlesex, England
Penguin Books Inc., 7110 Ambassador Road,
Baltimore, Maryland 21207, U.S.A.
Penguin Books Australia Ltd, Ringwood,
Victoria, Australia

First published 1971
Copyright © Ivan Butler, 1971

Made and printed in Great Britain by
Cox & Wyman Ltd, London, Reading
and Fakenham
Set in Intertype Times

For Francis

Contents

List of Illustrations

Preface

This book is compiled mainly from personal interviews. As far as possible I have retained the speaker's own words, editing and condensing where necessary, but preserving, I hope, the flavour of each individual conversation. I have deliberately not attempted to reconcile conflicting opinions or even statements of fact; the book is intended as a documentary rather than a textbook.

Although conditions of film-making may be changing considerably, with the decline of the factory studio, the growth of independent production, the emergence of the underground cinema, and the development of documentary in its widest sense, it seems to me that the large-scale feature film, whether or not it is used as a vehicle for significant comment beyond its own narrative interest, is likely to remain for some time yet the basis of the commercial cinema. My purpose is to provide an account of the processes involved in the making of feature films *today*, primarily in Britain and in the United States, and thus all the contributors to the book are active at the present time, and some are still comparatively young. Specific films are referred to only when they illustrate some particular point, and not because they either possess or lack merit.

Each chapter in the book deals with a particular job in the

process of film-making. This division of chapters is in some cases unavoidably arbitrary, since the jobs often overlap: for example, a producer, a writer, or a cameraman may also direct, an actor may also produce, a director may also act. The direct 'question and answer' presentation would have proved monotonous if I had used it throughout the book, but in two chapters, 'The Scriptwriter' and 'The Director', where the points raised were a matter of individual opinion, it seemed the most satisfactory method.

Acknowledgements

I should like to thank Alan Sawford-Dye of Associated British Elstree Studios, Brian Baxter of the British Film Institute, Chris Greenwood of Rogers, Cowan & Brenner, Theo Cowan, and Carolyn Pfeiffer for their help in arranging interviews; Kevin Gough-Yates and David Gladwell for permission to quote from an article in *Screen*; David Gordon for permission to quote from an article on the financing of British films published in *The Economist*, 8 March 1969; Fred T. Kennedy, General Manager of Central Casting; and particularly the large number of personal secretaries who paved my way into the presence of very busy and sometimes elusive people. Grateful thanks also to Nikos Stangos for advice and encouragement throughout, and to my wife for her patient help in checking and correcting the proofs. My greatest debt is to all those people engaged in the making and presentation of films who so generously gave me their time and attention, and who responded to my requests with readiness, interest and enthusiasm.

Ivan Butler
September 1970

Introduction

'It takes five men to make a movie,' states Kenneth MacGowan in *Behind the Screen*, using the word 'make' in the sense of 'give the work form'. The five are: producer, writer, director, cutter (editor) and cameraman. But the genesis of every film, whether it is a one-minute shot or a four-hour epic, is an idea in the mind of just one person: a producer, a director, a reader, a star, a literary agent or a scout may see in a novel, short story or play certain screen possibilities, or an author may be working on a book with screen adaptation in mind.

Whoever has the original idea for a film, it is soon taken away from him. The differences between inception, realization and experience in a film, however modest in scale, and in other forms of the arts, are very great. A novelist writes down the words his reader will eventually see; the publisher and the printer may affect the outward appearance of the book, but not, to any great extent, the content. An artist puts paint on to the canvas, and the result is exactly as it will be seen in a gallery, although the painting's placing and lighting may have some effect. A composer's notes are preserved in his score, but he depends on a single interpreter or on a number of performers led by a conductor, and the readings may vary considerably. The playwright is further removed from direct personal control; the producer, actors, scenic designers, electricians, and finally the audience itself all have a share in the result, and the printed play differs greatly from the live performance. In the film, however, the differences are greater still.

A feature film is a corporate, rather than even a group, undertaking. The number of people on location during shooting for John Huston's *The Misfits* '... was over 200 people, including 4 on the camera, 5 on sound, 8 on lighting, 5 on props, 3 on set decoration, a painter, a greenman (fake shrubs, etc.), a doctor, a masseur, a dialogue director, a script girl and a script man, 4 secretaries, a production assistant, 2 assistant directors, a personal maid for Miss Monroe, a make-up man for each of the principals, a body make-up girl, a hairdresser, a stand-in for each actor, doubles for the rougher scenes (including a double for Clark Gable's double), a still photographer, a publicity assistant, a dramatic coach, an auditor, an assistant auditor, a transportation chief, 20 local drivers, 3 pilots, 10 cowboys, a rodeo clown, 6 policemen, 3 watchmen, 2 dogs and their trainer, 5 stockmen with horses and bulls, a wardrobe man and woman, a seamstress, an assistant film editor, a 5-man catering service, a whistle blower, plus various baby-sitters for the men who had brought their wives and children.'[1]

The tree-like chart (p. 15), compiled by Alan Sawford-Dye, is a diagram of the growth of the average feature film, from its beginnings in the script to its final version on the screen, showing the role of each person or department concerned, and the proportion of time during which each is likely to be actively involved. With so many parts it seems at first sight astonishing that a coherent whole could ever result, let alone a work of art.

Whether or not the film is an 'art form' has been discussed for a long time. Ultimately the answer depends, it seems to me, very much on a definition. 'What is art?' is a question to which there can be as many answers as there are artists or even art-lovers. The fact that many people, rather than just one 'creator', are involved in the making of a feature film need not preclude

1. From a report by James Goode, quoted in *John Huston, King Rebel*, by William F. Nolan, Los Angeles, 1965

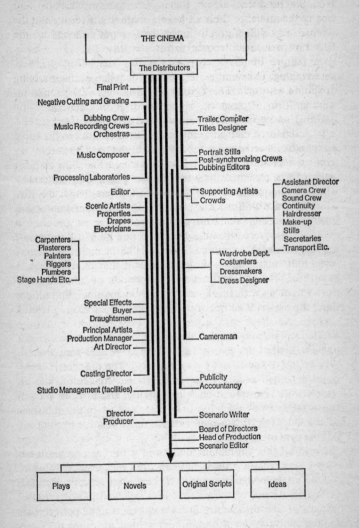

it from being a work of art. Except to the expert who can conjure up a musical or theatrical performance in his imagination,
a score or play-script on a shelf is as dormant as a roll of film
in a can: it is only brought to life by the collaboration of a
large number of people. Indeed, the film may be said to have
an advantage over music and drama, for once completed, it is,
or should be, unalterable (except by variations in projection or
wear and tear of the print, which are, of course, extremely important), and unable to be manipulated by 'interpreters'.

In practice, of course, as many a filmgoer knows to his fury,
inexcusable liberties are often taken with the finished film in the
form of unauthorized and indiscriminate cutting. The responsibility for such mutilations is almost impossible to pin down;
when the subject is raised, the production company, the distributor, the exhibitor, the projectionist, all claim innocence.
Following a complaint from an irate patron recently, a cinema
manager discovered that the copy of a film he had been showing was twenty-three minutes short, and badly out of synchronization although one would have thought that the film should
have been checked beforehand. Thousands of cinema-goers
have to put up with this kind of arbitrary manipulation all the
time; the majority do not even know that the carefully planned
rhythm and shape of a sequence has been ruined, or that the
projection is wrong, or that the colour is not what the director
had originally intended. A foreign-language film runs the additional risk of damage by poor dubbing. The practice is sometimes defended as a necessary evil, but as Alec Guinness says,
'One's voice is a part of one's personality, and obviously when
this is taken away much has to be lost, even when the dubber is
very good. Only half a performance remains – it's like cutting
out the eyes of an actor.'

From all this, the unique quality of a film as *one* work becomes apparent: it is the combined work of a great number of
people all involved in a more or less creative capacity. The
following studies of the various jobs involved in the complex
process of film-making are in no way meant to be prescriptive.
On the contrary, the information presented, including the interviews and statements given by the people concerned, is purely

descriptive of the processes which are employed, for better or for worse, in the making of feature films today, mostly in Britain. The aim of the book is to describe systematically the inner workings of the film industry in the words of its own workers, and acquaint a large public with the jobs involved.

Two things emerge clearly from the interviews and statements that follow: first, that all the members of the vast team working on a feature film have one aim, that the film they are making should be the 'best possible' of its kind; and second, that however diversified the work, the efforts of all involved are combined to one end – the vision of the director. But as the director himself would be the first to admit, his vision, in so complex a medium, can remain only visionary without the creative contributions of his collaborators.

Once the feature film is completed, the entertainment industry has different and more practical concerns. Work of art or mere entertainment (or both), a feature film costs a great deal of money. It is made to be sold, to be brought to the attention of the public for whose consumption it has been produced. In this respect, whether one approves or not, the fact remains that the feature film is – for the present at least – primarily a commercial consumer product. As one of the directors interviewed in this book says, 'What is the use of the most high-minded film if, because the makers have forgotten they are working in a mass-entertainment medium, it plays to empty seats?'

1. The Producer
(Executive Producer, Associate Producer,
Production Manager)

Many people, even within the film industry itself, have a con-
fused idea of the producer's proper function. In theory, the
producer's job is to supervise the film's finances – to attend to
the business side while the director attends to the artistic: in
practice, however, the job often involves far more than this.

In the 'great days' of Hollywood the producer was an employee, an administrator, assigned to a particular film by the
studio to watch how the money was spent. With the decline of
the big companies came the growth of the independent producer, a man generally responsible for the whole organization
of the film – obtaining the finance, finding the story, (or 'property'), choosing the director, the cast, the cameraman and the
technicians. Now, the director is becoming more and more the
'man in charge', and may act as his own producer, or engage a
producer to work for him.

Let us first consider, however, the producer as king, or perhaps more correctly, as president. Carl Foreman traces the
growth of the independent producer of feature films, and also
the development of his own company:

'Historically it *all* began as independent production – scores
of independent producers all on their own, in and around New

York. Shortly afterwards, many went to California to escape from private monopolies. There, companies began to merge into major studios: MGM, Paramount, RKO, etc., and independent production went out of the window. Producers became employees, working on a salary, receiving no percentage of profits, but also incurring no risk. Some of them rose to great stature, but they still remained employees. The change began to take shape after the Second World War. A group of important American directors, Frank Capra, George Stevens and William Wyler, decided to form an independent company called Liberty Films, together with a producer, Samuel Briskin, as overall administrative head. The situation was similar to that of the formation by Chaplin, Fairbanks, Mary Pickford and D. W. Griffith of the original United Artists in the 1920s, although United Artists had by this time ceased functioning as such and was solely a distributing concern. When Liberty Films was eventually sold, other companies were formed. I became friendly with Stanley Kramer in the Signal Corps of the US Army and we joined forces with one or two other young film-makers and produced a number of successful movies such as *Home of the Brave* (1949, directed by Mark Robson), *Champion* (1949, directed by Mark Robson), *The Men* (1950, directed by Fred Zinnemann) and, in particular, *High Noon* (1952, directed by Fred Zinnemann). The success of these pictures gave an impetus to the whole movement, and now almost every one of the big distributing companies will make deals with independent producers.'

The independence of an independent producer, of course, varies. Foreman is managing director of a company which has had a long-term arrangement with Columbia Pictures since 1958. Choice of subject is a matter of agreement: contractually, as distributors Columbia have the right to turn away any suggestion, but in fact they have never done so. Once the subject is approved, Foreman has complete right of approval over the screenplay. 'This is unusual,' he says. 'As a rule an independent producer must find a backer who likes his script.' Columbia also has the right to reduce the estimated cost of a production in

the matter of casting the stars. Once all this is settled, and the
director and leading members of the unit engaged, the film is
budgeted. Columbia supplies the whole of the finance; profits, if
any, are split. Columbia, as distributors as well as backers, are
responsible for advertising and publicity, and for selling the
picture when completed. As distributors they first recoup this
expenditure (which is not part of the 'negative' cost, i.e. the
actual cost of making the film) by deducting their commission
from the box office receipts. The balance of the receipts after
deduction of such expenses then goes to recover the 'negative'
cost until such time as, everyone hopes, this is wiped out and
profits begin to mount up. As producer, Foreman receives a fee,
and is paid nothing more until all these expenses have been
covered. He then takes a percentage of any further in-
comings.

With minor variations, this is the general procedure in all
independent productions. The producer may or may not receive
a fee as well as a percentage, or his fee may be deferred.

'The position in England,' Foreman comments, 'was more
difficult for some independent producers because the financial
sources were not so numerous. Many projects never got off the
ground because the distributing company was only willing to
put up 70 per cent of the budget and the producer himself had
to try to find the rest. The National Film Finance Corporation
was set up by the British Government to supply the missing
capital provided they approved of the film, but it is important
to note that the 70 per cent had to come first, either from a
distributing company or the banks. Then a few years ago the
arrival of American interests and investment in British film-
making changed the situation considerably. It ran into high
gear after the success of *The Bridge on the River Kwai* (1957,
director David Lean), a key film in the encouragement of American investment. Columbia, who backed *Kwai*, had already
made one or two fairly successful films over here. I owned the
rights and had written the screenplay. This was sold to Sam
Spiegel, who had decided to make films in Britain. Columbia
put up the money, and the rest is cinema history.'

The producer's role in the actual making of a film varies
enormously. He may confine himself completely to the administrative side; if he has technical knowledge, he may be present
before, during and after shooting; he may be a man with a
flair for finding subjects but little technical knowledge; he may
be a man of great artistic sensitivity. Producers can leave as
strong a personal imprint on the finished product as the director
himself.

Ivan Foxwell, who started work as a camera assistant at the
age of twenty, is, for example, an independent producer who
takes a particularly active share in the creative work on his
films. Foxwell, like Foreman, owns his own company, which is
financed up to 100 per cent by a major distributor.

'The distributor pays me a substantial fee and a percentage of
the profits. This is not as easy as it sounds – everything depends
on the past record of the producer. As with most producers
nowadays, I sign a separate contract for each film.

'The first thing, of course, is to find a "property" – the term
in cinema circles for a story, play, idea, theme – on which the
film is to be based. At this stage I will spend four or more
hours every day just reading. Publishers send books to film
producers or companies in either manuscript or page-proof
form. The rights to the property are secured and then the story
is developed in conjunction with a writer and a director. I
bought the film rights of *The Quiller Memorandum* (1966, directed by Michael Anderson) while it was still in typescript. In
the case of a book which had been published for some years,
Evelyn Waugh's *Decline and Fall* (filmed under the title *Decline and Fall ... of a Birdwatcher* in 1968, directed by John
Krish), I set out on paper how I thought it would work as a
film, because obviously a book like that had been passed up by
other people for a number of years, and then submitted my
ideas to Twentieth Century Fox, who then purchased it.

'The next step is to interest the right director and the appropriate writer to turn the property into a film script – and also to
have someone in mind for the leading parts. The writer builds
up his screenplay in consultation with the director and myself.
A first draft is finished and submitted to the distributor. Mean-

while I line up the main members of the cast and technicians. Eventually a date is set to start production. This may depend on a whole variety of conflicting considerations – the availability of a particular studio, the freedom of a star from other commitments, the suitability (it is hoped) of weather conditions – often a producer's worst headache. In *Decline and Fall . . . of a Birdwatcher*, for instance, we were particularly unlucky with bad weather, but the one day we needed a downpour to drown out the school sports – the sun shone!'

The choice of a studio depends largely on the type of film to be made. One studio may have a very good tank for battles and storms, another an exceptionally useful street or town square for exteriors. A company will often make one studio its base and hire others for special scenes. The studio supplies all equipment, stage space, and their own staff: the producer brings his own lighting cameraman, art director, and editor, 'casting' them as he does his stars.

A producer may form a company for the purpose of making a single film, after which it will be disbanded. Often a 'package deal' is made up, usually comprising story, director and star; this is offered to a distributing company. Frequently the name of the star is the deciding factor; few financing companies are prepared to make the enormous outlay of money necessary unless there is a 'box-office name' available – thus confuting the assertion that the star system is dead. Top-ranking stars earn more money and wield more influence than ever before.

Views differ on the increasing tendency nowadays for directors, stars, and writers to combine producing with their own jobs. Ivan Foxwell and Arthur Jacobs consider that producer and director need each other to consult and 'bounce ideas back and forth'. Carl Foreman, on the other hand, is all in favour of combining the functions of producer and director. On *The Victors* (1965), which he wrote, produced and directed, he comments: 'It was a great physical and mental strain. It's not all that fun to be absolutely alone – with nobody to discuss things with. All the same, I find it immensely exhilarating to have it all to myself.'

The producer's personal staff may number up to ten people,

responsible for the schedule and budget of the entire concern. Frequent meetings with the production or distributing company, and innumerable inter-office consultations, are necessary. Working closely with the producer is the associate producer. Roy Baird describes his job and responsibilities:

'When a producer is also the director of a film, he has no time to attend to the financial details. He goes to Paramount or Columbia with his script. They say, "Yes, you can have a million dollars," then it's handed to me to sort out. I am a sort of liaison officer between the producer/director and the company, and am in effect responsible for seeing that the limit of expenditure is fixed. I work out the entire first budget, estimating every single item of expense. This also entails working out the schedule so that studio space is used to best advantage, expensive stars' time is not wasted, etc. Then I go to the distributor, and the whole plan is worked over with an expert. It's also my part to contract the artists, other than the stars, and the technicians. I watch over the finances during shooting, editing, dubbing, everything, in fact, until the film is delivered to the distributor – and sometimes afterwards, chasing up the advertising and exploitation.'

Also on the producer's staff are a production manager, who deals with the daily running of the production, engaging the unit, checking time sheets, stores, etc., and a production accountant who makes a cost statement each week.

Expenditure is divided into two sections, 'above and below the line'. Above the line are the director's and producer's fees, the fees for the story and script rights, and the payments to the stars. These are the costliest single items, all of them negotiable, and sometimes deferred. Below the line comes everything else – the payments to the remainder of the cast, and to the technicians; studio expenses; catering, transport and housing on location; the thousand and one items which are 'direct cost', and cannot be argued over. Also to be taken into account is the break factor, which averages 2.4 per cent of the negative cost of the film. This means that if the film costs, say, £100,000 it will have to earn £240,000 – allowing for such post-production items as distribution charges and print costs – before it will begin to show a profit.

Case Histories of Three Films

Arthur P. Jacobs on *Planet of the Apes*
(1967, directed by Franklin Schaffner).

'I was in Paris during the filming of *What a Way to Go,* when I met a literary agent. He told me about a superb new book by Pierre Bouille, author of *The Bridge on the River Kwai*. It was still in manuscript, and in French, so I was told the outline and the highlights. I thought, great! I took it to Richard Zanuck. He thought it was too far out. To Jack Warner – too far out. I contacted Blake Edwards as director. He thought it was great. Charlton Heston as star. *He* thought it was great. Still – no! All the companies turned it down. Everybody going around as apes? Ridiculous! I had six artists do paintings of the apes – the sixth was good. I went back to Zanuck – no! Edward G. Robinson said he would play an ape. Heston made a special ten-minute test. Zanuck took his office staff along – the reaction was good. We were on! The ending was my own idea. In the book, the Heston character returned to earth, opened the door at the airport, and found everyone was an ape. I knew that ending would be guessed by the audience. The new one meant a terrific change. In the first version we could have used cars and other familiar sights, simply because Heston was *not* on the earth. Now the place must not look like the earth, but must have sufficient resemblance for the ending to be plausible. No one noticed that there was no apparent source of light during the night scenes – no lamps or anything. Working on the shock ending, which had to be as strong as *Citizen Kane's* "Rosebud", was a problem. A group of us were sitting in a New York café discussing it, when suddenly I noticed the decorations round the wall – the Statue of Liberty. I pointed and said, "that's it!" The most costly item in the film, incidentally, was the make-up for the apes.'

Anthony Simmons on *Four in the Morning* (1963-5).

'Although I was actually the director of this film, with John Morris as my producer, I was intimately concerned with both sides of the project. Our original idea was to make a kind of old-fashioned lyrical documentary about the River Thames. Then, as we began to shoot, I decided to develop the story, basing it on an old Victorian poem about a girl who was found dead in the river. I discussed the project with actors and expanded the basic idea into a fuller treatment dealing with the two lovers. The details of this story – the unmarried couple, played by Ann Lynn and Brian Phelan – were created almost entirely by improvisation. Together with the producer and cameraman we formed a company and approached the National Film Finance Corporation for backing for what was intended as a fifty-minute film. They said they needed something more substantial, and this led to my writing the husband and wife story. This gave us a pattern where we had two stories, one dealing with a married woman, the other with a bachelor girl, with the story of the suicide as a link or chorus between them. The NFFC then agreed to put up 80 per cent of the cash. Later, as production grew, the NFFC agreed to a higher budget, but on the basis of £1 from them to match £1 from us, although our part did not necessarily have to be found all in cash, but could take the form of facilities, deferred salaries, and so on.

'The entire film was shot on location, most of the husband and wife story in a Putney house. The ground floor became our office, the second floor the set, and the top our store-room, cluttered with lighting and sound equipment. The two main stories were filmed separately to fit in with the artists' availability. We shot half the first story and then had to wait until Ann Lynn became free again from TV commitments. Then we waited another two months until Judi Dench was free to start the second story. The linking narrative about the suicide was completed in five days shooting. Our first plan for editing was to run the two stories consecutively with the suicide as an introduction and epilogue. We hated the effect and decided to experiment with intercutting them into a sort of mosaic. The recutting was done in thirty-six hours.

'The finished film took considerably longer to launch than it did to make. We gave one show to about seventy people to test audience reaction. It was tremendous, but we had no distribution and no backing. We tried to enter it for the main Cannes Festival unsuccessfully, but fortunately someone from the Paris magazine *Arts* had seen it, and arranged a Cannes showing for us outside the festival at an off-peak hour. To our surprise we had an audience of more than 600. We managed to win the 'Prix de Cinema d'Art et d'Essai'. The film was immediately invited to other festivals. We accepted Locarno, where we eventually won the Grand Prix. By this time we had signed a contract with a distribution company, Connoisseur, and a release date was fixed with the Cameo Group. In fact the opening was delayed for a further six months, and was then fixed for the worst week of the year – the week before Christmas. Frankly, we expected disaster, but the film ran to full evening houses for more than three months. It has since played over 200 cinemas in Britain, mostly with *The War Game* (1965, directed by Peter Watkins), but has only played occasionally in cinemas belonging to the main circuits. In Paris it did well despite a heat wave. In Israel it played for months. In Germany it was shown dubbed on television. It was sold on very good terms to America, but met with resistance from the cinemas and so far has not been released.'

Richard Attenborough on *Oh! What a Lovely War* (1969)

'The financial set-up for the film was unique. The normal method in this country is a 100 per cent financial deal by a distributor, who puts up the entire money, gives the production company a percentage of the profits and owns the project outright the moment it is delivered. In the case of *Oh! What a Lovely War*, it was my first picture as a director, it was a subject which had none of the supposed prerequisites of a commercial enterprise – other than the stars – no story line, no main character with which an audience could identify, no sex, no violence ... so one was very apprehensive about one's ability to raise sufficient money. However, after discussions with Len Deighton and Brian Duffy, who had bought the film rights from Joan Littlewood, it was decided to go to George H. Ornstein, who was at that time in charge of production for Paramount in England, and who had already pioneered such films as *Tom Jones,* the Beatles films and the Bond films. Ornstein felt a degree of apprehension, but was prepared to promote the idea to the head of Paramount, Charles Bluhdorn. A meeting was arranged at which, since Bluhdorn had neither seen the stage production nor read the script, I acted out some sequences from the film and also sang some of the songs. By the end of this he was greatly intrigued, and quite touched by certain sequences, and I told him I could get a number of stars to play guest spots – Olivier and eight or ten others. He said, "You couldn't really get eight or ten," and I said I could – he said they would all want phenomenal salaries and I said no, they would work for token amounts. Then he asked if I could guarantee him five, including Olivier, and I said yes, I could. He asked how much money I wanted and I told him $2\frac{1}{2}$ to 3 million dollars. Len Deighton, Brian Duffy and myself were prepared to work for nothing, and put the scriptwriting in for nothing, provided Paramount were prepared to make no overhead charges whatever. (Overhead charges can range from 5 per cent to 25 per cent, which on a budget of, say, 2,000,000 dollars could be terrifying.)

'Charles Bluhdorn said "Okay", and we had a deal. In effect we ran over to 3,100,000 dollars, and also went somewhat over schedule – about six seconds per day over what I thought we would be – partly on account of meeting with some very bad weather. We received the extra money from Paramount without question, and experienced no interference in any way over the production.

'In exchange for our taking no money whatever for the making of the film, the three of us were allotted 60 per cent (in place of the usual 40 per cent or 50 per cent) of the profits of the picture – if and when they arrive. Roughly, you have to work on a 2.5 per cent ratio of the negative cost: if a picture costs, say, $3,000,000, you have to take $7,500,000 *return to the distributors* (the distributors' gross, which pays for the distribution charge, the prints, the exploitation, advertising, etc., etc.) before the profits start to come in. This means that *Oh! What a Lovely War* will have to take something like $7,500,000 before I receive a dollar.'

Film Production Finance in Various Countries

The subject of motion picture financing in different countries is an exceedingly complex and shifting one, and a complete survey of it would require far more space than is available here. In the United Kingdom, the NFFC was set up, in 1949, to provide short-term backing. Apart from the initial loan to the NFFC, the government aid the industry receives is through legislation rather than money.[1] Government support now takes three forms: quota, levy and the NFFC. The quota is 30 per cent. Every cinema must devote at least this much of its time to new British-made full-length films. However, films made here with American finance count as 'British' for quota purposes and the help the 'British cinema' (meaning film-makers) thus derives is therefore limited. The levy is about 6 per cent of cinema takings, calculated according to a formula. Cinemas taking less than £400 a week are excluded. And, if necessary, the rate of levy will be reduced to ensure that not more than £5,000,000 altogether is raised in any one year. This money goes to the British Film Fund Agency, which, after paying running expenses and a grant to the Children's Film Foundation, hands out the rest of the revenue to producers of 'British films', in proportion to takings. *Thunderball* grossed a fifth of the takings of all 'British films' in 1965 and so collected a fifth of the fund. Mention should also be made of the British Film Institute's Production Board, which financed, among other films, *Herostratus* (1967, directed by Don Levy).

It is often believed that in America the bankers who loan the money to finance film production influence picture content or

1. I am indebted to David Gordon for the following details, published in an article in *The Economist*, 8 March 1969.

film company policies. 'This is really a myth,' says Jack Valenti. A. H. Howe, Vice-President of the Bank of America, which for years has advanced funds for productions, deals with this 'myth' out of his own knowledge and experience.[2]

'You have often heard it said that certain stars are bankable. You have been told that pictures were made or not made because bankers did or did not like the script. Rumours in the industry say that this company or that . . . are really controlled by the bankers and, of course, this accounts for these companies' sad showings. All of these are myths which just aren't so. . . . There are no bankable stars! I can hear you say, "You mean that if I brought you Elizabeth Taylor and Richard Burton, it wouldn't make any difference?" Of course it would make a difference; but in view of the higher costs these top people would automatically bring with them, their participation is no assurance that a production loan would be repaid from film revenue alone. This is true of every combination of actor and actress, writer, director and producer, regardless of past records, hits or awards. Each new picture is a new venture, and a loan must be so arranged that it will be repaid even in the event of a disaster.

'It follows then that the banker does not even try to influence production decisions as to what pictures are made. His effort is directed to ensure repayment of the loan; he lets the people in the business pick the packages . . .

'It is the distributor who takes the risk. He is the one to whom each new package must be sold. He is the one who dictates certain ingredients, who furnishes a guarantee of completion and puts up the funds if the picture goes over budget. He is the one who takes a distribution fee of 30 to 35 per cent of the distributor's gross, which if he is very lucky compensates him for the losses on the pictures which do not return their production cost. . . . The distributors take the risks of the production cost in perhaps 90 per cent of the dollars involved in picture-making. The rest is taken by the occasional producer

2. The extracts which follow are from a long article by A. H. Howe in the *Journal of the Producers Guild of America*, March 1969. I am indebted to Jack Valenti for bringing this important survey to my attention.

who can and is willing to back his judgement with his own assets, or by other investors brought in by the producer.

'Where does the bank come in? It usually furnishes the money. It evaluates the assets of those who take the risk, and makes loans based on the picture, but backstopped by the risk takers ...

'When you [the producer] have found your risk taker, an entity which is willing to back you with its financial strength, the ease with which you obtain a bank loan depends upon the credit standing of that risk taker ...

'When granted, your loan will be patterned to permit borrowing of funds from the bank for production as needed and repayment from the producer's share of distribution proceeds, assuming the picture is successful ...

'[The basic organization of the loan] is a rather simple transaction, but such loans often breed extreme complexities as they progress. Obviously, over-budget expenditures require action by the completion guarantor and, if the excess costs are serious enough, will sometimes result in takeover of control of production by representatives of the risk taker.

'If distributor results are unfavourable, the distributor will be asked to furnish estimates of future returns and if these are insufficient to pay the loan, additional payments, even before maturity, may be required ...

'The future of the motion picture industry lies in the hands of those who conceive the projects, put together the difficult ingredients, and follow through to the finished product – the producers. If [the producer] can add to all these cares a realistic evaluation risk and a sure knowledge of the financial facts of life, his batting average in the years ahead is certain to improve. And, his banker will always be eager to help.'

Government subsidies are available for feature film production in most of the countries of Western Europe.[3] West Germany, Sweden (through the Swedish Film Institute), Den-

3. The following details are taken from a comparative chart dealing with conditions in Western Europe, published in the British quarterly *Sight and Sound* in 1966/7.

mark (at script stage, through the Danish Film Fund), and
Spain all offer direct grants. In France there is a system of aid
based on box-office returns; this is, of course, a post-production
grant, the rate of which increases with the commercial success
of the film. Similarly, Italy subsidizes to a certain percentage a
producer whose project satisfies stated conditions, basing the
amount on box-office takings; there is also a special fund for
grants towards interest payment on loans for production
finance.

In the cases of France, Italy, West Germany, Sweden and
Denmark, grants are financed either from entertainment tax or
from a levy on cinema tickets; in the case of Spain, from dubbing rights paid for the circulation of foreign films in Spanish
versions.

In the Communist countries, film production comes under
government control and is part of the cultural organization of
the state, the degree of freedom varying in time and place in
accordance with the political mood. In Russia, actors receive a
yearly salary from the Soviet Government, plus a bonus for
good work, and in general this salary improves with the grade
assigned to the actor by the state.

Some Comparative Cost Figures

The following list of films gives an indication of the approximate cost involved in the making of feature films. Most of the
films have been made in the past five or six years, but one or two
earlier ones are included for comparison.

	$
Twelve Angry Men (1957)	343,000
(Sidney Lumet estimates that the cost today would be about $600,000)	
Carry On – Up the Khyber (1968)	480,000
Oedipus the King (1967)	500,000
A Midsummer Night's Dream (1968)	500,000
If . . . (1968)	500,000
High Noon (1952)	800,000
Otley (1968)	1,100,000
The Deadly Affair (1966)	1,250,000

	$
Born Free (1965)	1,400,000
From Here to Eternity (1953)	1,900,000
Intolerance (1916)	1,900,000
Decline and Fall . . . of a Birdwatcher (1968)	2,000,000
A Man for All Seasons (1966)	2,000,000
The Fixer (1968)	2,100,000
The Manchurian Candidate (1962)	2,400,000
The Group (1965)	2,400,000
The Quiller Memorandum (1966)	3,000,000
Oh! What a Lovely War (1969)	3,100,000
The Train (1964)	4,500,000
Mayerling (1968)	5,000,000
The Guns of Navarone (1961)	5,500,000
Planet of the Apes (1967)	5,800,000
The Charge of the Light Brigade (1968)	6,000,000
Grand Prix (1966)	10,500,000
Ben Hur (1959)	15,000,000
Cleopatra (1963)	37,000,000

2. The Scriptwriter

Every feature film starts from a story and every story needs to be prepared for film production. The producer, having decided on his original idea, or the novel or play to be adapted, calls in the scriptwriter.

In the old Hollywood days, although big literary names were sometimes brought in at enormous fees, the scriptwriter was often a regular employee. Many studios had rows of writers in little boxes, each tapping away to order on his typewriter; it was very much a hack job. There is a well-known story of a Hollywood producer who flung open the door of one little box, threw down a bundle of three or four rejected stories, and instructed the occupant: 'Stick all these together and make some sort of story out of them.' The position of the scriptwriter is different today. He is recognized as an important member of the creative hierarchy: producer/director/scriptwriter/lighting cameraman/ art director. He is contracted for a particular film, and may be approached by the company or by an independent producer assembling a package deal; often he is personally asked for by the director. There have been some notable director/ writer teams, for example Frank Capra and Robert Riskin, John Ford and Dudley Nichols, Marcel Carné and Jacques Prévert, Billy Wilder and I. A. L. Diamond or Charles Brackett.

A scriptwriter is often asked to prepare a script long before a project has got off the ground, perhaps even before it has been planned. For instance, Paul Dehn has already written and been paid for a film script for *Macbeth* which, it is hoped, Richard Burton and Elizabeth Taylor will one day produce.

Although there are many methods of procedure, the following is the most usual one. The writer receives an advance for a first draft of his screenplay. (There used to be a preliminary outline called a treatment, but this is going out of use.) Very often the scriptwriter is the first person to receive remuneration from the producer himself. He is then given a deadline by which to produce the draft. If the company or the producers reject the draft script, the matter goes no further. If they approve, the scriptwriter is contracted for the rest of the work, a final sum being paid on the commencement of shooting. Any further necessary work will be paid for by arrangement, either by the week or 'on call'. Occasionally top rank writers receive a percentage of the profits or alternatively, the writer may ask for a smaller initial sum and a percentage.

Scripts generally involve three stages of progression: outline, screenplay with dialogue and essential action, and shooting script with camera angles, etc. Very often, however, the producer, director and sometimes the composer and art director will discuss the idea for a film at great length with the scriptwriter, before even the outline is written.

Paul Dehn

Paul Dehn wrote the scripts for *Seven Days to Noon* (with James Bernard, 1951); *Orders to Kill* (1958); *Goldfinger* (with Richard Maibaum, 1964); *The Spy Who Came in from the Cold* (1964); *The Deadly Affair* (1965); *The Taming of the Shrew* (1965); *Beneath the Planet of the Apes* (1969); *Fragment of Fear* (1970).

You came to scriptwriting from film criticism: how did the change come about?

I decided to write a film script in order to increase my armoury as a critic. I thought that, to be able to allocate praise or blame justly, I should have some practical knowledge of how a film came into being. So I wrote a film treatment of an original story, *Seven Days to Noon* (1951, directed by John Boulting). It won me a Hollywood Oscar. I went on to write further scripts, documentaries, another feature, *Orders to Kill* (1958, directed by Anthony Asquith), but still for the purpose of improving myself as a critic. Eventually, owing to changes in the newspaper world, and an offer to collaborate on the script for *Goldfinger* (1964, directed by Guy Hamilton), I gave up criticism and took to full-time screenwriting.

How do you set about adapting a novel, such as The Spy Who Came in from the Cold *or* The Deadly Affair? *Do you refer much to the original book, or to the author?*

I soak myself in the book and always secure the author's reactions to my first draft screenplay – if he's alive. The big problem with a novel such as *The Spy* is that so much of the story unfolds in the mind of the hero. Short of using 'voice-over' technique, which I detest, I had to sit down and work out a complicated cross, double-cross situation without any extra character for the protagonist to confide in. Fortunately for this particular case, Richard Burton is excellent at revealing his thoughts without verbally expressing them.

What about adapting Shakespeare – the question of substituting 'business' for lines?

Every stage producer cuts Shakespeare. No film director ever excelled Sir Herbert Tree at replacing lines by business or spectacle. *The Taming of the Shrew* (filmed under Franco Zeffirelli's direction, 1967) is eminently cuttable. All the extra action we put in was actually described in the play or could legitimately be imagined to have taken place. The wedding scene was pure Zeffirelli, but the account of the off-stage catastrophe is all there in the play. Any changes we made were faithful to the 'spirit of Shakespeare'.

So many people think that scriptwriting is nothing but dialogue. This is nonsense. When I was working on *Macbeth* I was asked, even by those in the trade, 'What are you going to do, except edit and rearrange? Shakespeare's already written it.' In fact, I have done an enormous amount of work, of which I hope Shakespeare would approve. Take the witches as an

example. I suddenly realized that the familiars of all three
witches are mentioned, but not elaborated: the toad, the owl,
Graymalkin the cat. It occurred to me that each witch adopted
the mannerisms of her own familiar. Even the lines spoken by
each witch suggested the likeness to the animal concerned. It
immediately became clear that I could hint on the screen at the
omnipresence of the witches by using the familiars. This I attempted to do, and in the big final spell-casting scene, to make
the spell as potent as possible, I caused each witch actually to
drop her own familiar into the cauldron, for which there is
coincidental evidence in the text! In the end the three witches,
drained of power, leave the cavern and go off into the grey
Scottish dawn, traipsing across the moor with bundles on their
backs, a trio of harmless old women looking for another job.

How long does it take you to prepare a script?

About two months for a first draft, as a general rule.

*Do you work closely with the director from the preliminary
stages?*

I like to have the director in from the start. It saves endless
re-writes later.

*Do you insert into your final script such details as camera
angles?*

Yes, I do, because I *see* the script while I write it as if it was a
film projected on to a blank wall. Different directors, of
course, prefer different types of screenplays. Joseph Losey,
for instance, likes minimal technical details: the ideal
script for him is about 60 pages – the usual length is more
like 120 pages. Some scriptwriters also prefer to avoid
technicality. Frederic Raphael hates writing, 'We pull
back to reveal . . .' He leaves such things as camera movements
to the director, and writes more in master-scenes.

*Does the knowledge that a particular star is to play in one of
your films affect your writing of the script?*

Sometimes, and a change of cast can of course mean a
change of style. In *The Spy*, for instance: originally Burt Lancaster was to have played the lead. This would have involved a
somewhat different characterization, and Lancaster would have
had to play it in Irish instead of English.

Do you spend much time on the set once shooting has started?

It depends on the director. Zeffirelli, for example, improvises a great deal, on sudden whims. He prepares carefully, then may have an unexpected inspiration. It's helpful in such cases to have the writer around to work out a new idea. Personally I prefer to deliver the script and get on with another film. Sidney Lumet likes the writer to be at the first read-through and then get the hell out! Lumet, incidentally, is a marvellous director to write for. He is able to say what he wants articulately – always a great help!

Robert Bolt

Robert Bolt wrote the scripts for *Lawrence of Arabia* (1962); *Dr Zhivago* (1965); *A Man for All Seasons* (1967); *Ryan's Daughter* (1969).

Which do you find affords you the most artistic satisfaction, writing for the stage or for the screen?

Materially, you can earn a better living, and a more secure one, writing for the cinema. The money you can expect to receive from a film of average size is much more than that from a successful play – and the film writer is paid whether the film is a success or not. For a really outstanding hit in the theatre, of course, you will in the end make much more than from any picture – but it has to be a real sockeroo! The element of security constitutes the main difference.

It's generally taken for granted that the theatre is the superior art from the writer's point of view. In one important respect this is so. In the theatre the author is, generally speaking, almost totally responsible for what the audience feels. The words are the principal weapon in the hands of the actor. An author watching a play thinks, 'This is *my* work, those people are my interpreters.' In the cinema this is not the case. The contribution of the actors is much larger, for one simple reason – the close-up. A good actor in close-up can convey much more with his eyes, his expression, with tiny gestures, than with the words he is speaking. Also, of course, the director's part is very much greater in the cinema, because his camera moves and plays about, and – above all – cuts. The actual feat of juxtaposing two very different images is in itself an artistic act and can be so much more eloquent and significant than what is said that it takes prior place. This is why, if you are interested in the cinema, you want to know of a film not who wrote it, but who directed it. Well, clearly a work of art for which you feel yourself finally responsible is more satisfying to you as a creator than one to which you merely feel you have made a large contribution. To that extent theatre is the more satisfying medium, and a novel or poetry even more so. Still, there is another aspect which I personally find exciting in the cinema, and that is the size of the audience. The mere knowledge of the enormous number of people who will see a film I have written stimulates me a great deal.

People think it must be much easier to write a screenplay than a play for the stage because the means of story-telling are so varied and flexible. In fact it is a form which demands very great economy indeed, down to the last phrase of your dialogue lines, and still more, down to the last few frames of your visual effects. Film takes a lot longer to run than many people think. A scene of a train approaching a broken bridge and hurtling into a river, or of two men in a bar brewing up for a fight, may seem to last for a few seconds because it is so exciting, whereas in fact one-and-a-half minutes of screen time may have gone by.

With all this, however, the film when it appears is primarily the director's creation. On balance, therefore, I must say that the theatre is the more satisfactory medium for the writer – but the question is by no means as obvious as is often thought. The day of the cynical hack screenwriter has gone, and the importance of the writer to the cinema is becoming more and more recognized.

The story of T.E. Lawrence and the novel Dr Zhivago *were enormous canvases. How do you achieve the tremendous condensation required in such cases?*

You attack it with an axe, not a pair of scissors. If you took

the novel *Dr Zhivago* as it stands and treated it as a shooting
script incident by incident the resulting film would run at least
sixty hours. Therefore, in the film you can have only a
twentieth of the book – therefore, you have to turn it into
something not merely shorter, but quite different. What do you
do? First you must read, read and re-read the book – which
means it must be a book you admire and by which you are
excited or you could never do it. You then put the book on one
side. Once I had finished my readings I did not refer to *Zhivago*
more than a dozen times, and then only to verify some small
point. If you are going to reduce a book to a twentieth of its
length, you can't go snipping out pieces here and there, up to
nineteen twentieths. You have to take in and digest the whole
work to your own satisfaction and then say, 'Well, the
significant things, the mounting peaks which emerge from this
vast panorama are such-and-such incidents, moral points, political points, emotional points, and those are all I can deal with
in dramatic form – all I *should* deal with.' Then you lock the
book in a cupboard and re-tell the story – its significance rather
than a full sequence of events. Of course, you have other guide-
lines laid down for you. *Zhivago*, for example, is a sort of love
letter to the Russian landscape. Pasternak made a significant or
symbolic use of natural conditions prevailing in Russia, and I
attempted to follow him. Once the 'peaks' have emerged the
problem is how to link them. You are under the necessity of
inventing incidents which do not occur in the book – threads
which will draw together *rapidly* a number of themes, where
Pasternak might have taken ten chapters. Another point is that
you cannot take your dialogue from the novel to any extent.
The characters have to become your characters – you make
them your own, make them speak as you would have them
speak. You do all this, relying on the fact that you have *under-
stood* the book, that your feeling about it is an adequate and
accurate one. There is no other way of making such a radical
act of condensation.

In the case of *Lawrence of Arabia*, I did some background
reading, and very quickly stopped, because I found the authorities all contradicted one another, not only as regards opinions

but also on matters of fact. So I put aside my tottering pile of books and returned to *The Seven Pillars of Wisdom*, even though it contains long passages of dubious veracity. I told myself I couldn't just pick out at my own convenience what I thought might or might not be true. Either certain things happened or in some way he wished they had happened. Supposing them to be true, what sort of individual was he whose life could contain so many seemingly irreconcilable deeds, thoughts, moods, modes of action?

Do you prepare a very detailed script?

Yes, I do – including some camera work. But it is the director who then draws up a shooting script, in which every shot is described. I think my scripts are unusually detailed, and they couldn't be so if I didn't work in close cooperation with the director from start to finish. This cooperation is, to me at any rate, essential in the writing of a film. But it can be very wearing and isn't easy to achieve. There has to be mutual trust, liking, esteem, and a common purpose.

If you knew a particular star would be playing in a film would it alter the emphasis of your script?

Yes, inevitably. I'm always conscious that I'm writing lines for an actor to speak. In the play, *A Man for All Seasons*, I was not writing something which Sir Thomas More had said, or that I wished he had said, but something for an actor to say on the stage. When I'm writing for the stage I visualize a stage, not More's house in Chelsea. When I'm writing for the cinema I am seeing the screen and actors performing. Therefore if I knew the actor I should inevitably start writing to cover his weakness or exploit his strength as I saw them. I'm more conscious of this in the theatre than in the cinema, but in both I prefer to attempt to write a good acting part and then look round for the actor to perform it.

Do you come on the set or on location during shooting?

No. If the process I have described above has been properly followed through my presence ought not to be necessary. Mutual agreement between director and writer should have been arrived at by the shooting stage. It has its dangers too, because it is always possible that an actor might come to the writer and question some point, and then you would have two directors – or one and a half – whom he could play off against each other.

In writing a 'period' or a directly historical script have you any hesitation in distorting literal fact to achieve dramatic effect – and perhaps more depth of truth?

No – and yes. If you have to distort historical truth at all radically in order to bring out the moral or artistic truth you are trying to express, then you ought not to have taken a historical theme. You ought to have invented situations and characters where you have absolute control and can do what you like with them. I *think* that in the historical things I have written nothing happens which could not have happened, and going a little further, that for everything that does happen there are reasonable historical grounds. Suppose that I am writing a family scene about a historical figure. There is very rarely evidence to be drawn upon for such a scene, but I try to make his behaviour, and that of his intimates, consonant with what is known about both. In the case of public events I might, as in *Zhivago,* have to concentrate three years of political manoeuvring into one simple scene. That is distortion, and therefore not true, but as long as that one scene embodies the political marrow of those three years I would not feel that I was lying. On the other hand, I should consider it wrong to depart from historic truth if the result was something which could not possibly have happened.

In *A Man for All Seasons* I quite deliberately made the King several years younger than he in fact was at the time, because what I felt to be essential about his relationship with More was something which was much more obvious when the King was in his earlier years. I felt it justifiable to play about with the time scale, partly because it was kept vague (no ages were mentioned), and partly because it represented the truth, as I felt it, about their relationship.

I think you should not deal with a historical character unless you have fallen in love with him, as I did with More – with his exquisite combination of moral rigour and appetite for life. Then you have to heighten those aspects which have drawn you to him, because you have only two hours in which to present him, as against the years during which his family knew him. A distortion – but it is an inevitable factor in translating reality into art. You are not telling a lie if the person to whom you are speaking knows that you are presenting artistic fantasy rather than strict fact. I don't think, however, that this artistic licence extends to the point at which an author takes a historic figure, St Joan or Thomas More or St Francis, to illuminate a modern theme – to say something about communism for instance, or the rise of Nazism. If you use figures who rightly were reverenced (as More was) for their courage and merit, you belittle and obscure them by borrowing their actual suffering, heroism and greatness for some idea of your own.

Graham Greene

Graham Greene's filmed novels and screenplays include *This Gun for Hire* (1942); *The Ministry of Fear* (1943); *Confidential Agent* (1945); *The Man Within* (1946); *Brighton Rock* (1947); *The Fugitive* (1948); *The Fallen Idol* (1948); *The Third Man* (1949); *The Heart of the Matter* (1953); *The Stranger's Hand* (1958); *The End of the Affair* (1955); *The Quiet American* (1958); *Our Man in Havana* (1959); *The Comedians* (1967).

Do you prefer to work from original material, or from adaptations either of your own work or that of other writers?
Apart from my disastrous first script of a John Galsworthy short story, and a later script of Shaw's *St Joan* (filmed in 1957, directed by Otto Preminger), my screenwriting has been either original material or adaptations of my own novels or stories. I certainly prefer to work, as with *The Third Man* (1949, directed by Sir Carol Reed) from original material, or from a short story. Condensation is always dangerous, while expansion is a form of creation.
How full a script do you prepare?
I begin with a treatment containing a good deal of dialogue. In fact the published version of *The Third Man* was the treatment for the film. The treatment to my mind has to create the

characters and not simply recount the story. I have only once had to write a full shooting script, for *Brighton Rock* (1947, directed by John Boulting). My work finishes with the completed screenplay. This may very well contain suggestions for camera angles, etc., but to my mind for the author to attempt a full shooting script is a waste of time. This is the job of the director.

Do you work closely with the director in the early stages?

I work closely with the director from the very beginning. After the first period of discussion I usually go away to work by myself on certain sections and then bring them back for further discussion. How often the consultations with the director take place is a matter of geography. When I worked with Carol Reed on *Our Man in Havana* we occupied two bedrooms in the same hotel in Brighton with a sitting-room in between for the secretary, and I passed my material through the secretary to Carol and we discussed matters at lunchtime. This degree of closeness is not always possible.

Do you spend much time on the set during shooting?

It varies a great deal. With *Our Man in Havana* I spent about ten days at the beginning, but this was less for the sake of the script than to help with the political situation, as Castro's government had only been in power for four months. Of course, I had already done a reconnaissance with Carol Reed to Havana to discuss possible settings. In the case of *The Comedians* (1967, directed by Peter Glenville) I spent two weeks in Dahomey and I visited the studios occasionally in Nice and Paris, but this was mainly if not entirely for my own satisfaction. We had made the script, as we believed, sufficiently watertight to require no changes, but a screenwriter learns a great deal from watching the actual shooting.

Do you know who is to play the leading parts before you start work, and does this affect your treatment of a story – in the case of adaption, for instance?

In almost all cases I have known who was to play the lead, but I don't think I have ever altered the emphasis of a film to fit the star. It usually happens the other way around: one chooses the star to fit the film.

How long, on a rough average, does it take you to prepare a script?

It's difficult to say. I once did a rush job – *St Joan* – in six weeks, but I would say that four to six months were required after the preliminary discussions and after the general line has been agreed.

Ian La Frenais and Dick Clement

Ian La Frenais and Dick Clement wrote the scripts for *The Jokers* (1963); *Otley* (1968); *Hannibal Brooks* (1968).

Did you find your experience as writers of television series helpful when you turned to films?

It helped us in that it made us realize we could write as a collaboration. But writing for films is much more concise. Every line in a film has to have a point – preferably two. In a television script there is much more 'chat', and the director has probably only two or three sets to play around with. In a good film the excellence of the script's contribution will often pass unnoticed: on the other hand you'll see a film where a great deal of talent has gone into covering up the fact that there was nothing there to begin with. By the time the poverty of the script has become apparent a lot of money has been poured into the project and it's too late to withdraw. So it goes through. You can't do anything without a good script.

Do you consider it necessary to prepare a very detailed script?

All visual effects must be included, for instance a montage sequence – at least its general theme. Very often the most important portions of a script are those which contain no dialogue at all. We think the writer should put in only such camera angles as can affect the revelation he is trying to depict. For instance, it might be important to indicate that character A should not be in shot because you don't want an audience to know that it is to him that character B is speaking until a certain moment: or you might want a scene shot through a shop window so that the characters cannot be heard.

Does your work finish when shooting starts?

You never finish writing a film. Even on the floor you find that things which worked all right on paper don't do so in practice. If you're around, you can polish and improve, even later, during the post-synching stage. You might find in a party scene, for instance, that there's a gap where you need to put in an 'off' line (spoken by someone out of shot), or even one spoken by the actor when he's visible, but with his back to the camera. In *Otley* (1969, directed by Dick Clement), we added several lines during the dubbing, and changed one, bringing back the same actor to do it. Romy Schneider actually posted a line on tape from Germany, which we afterwards dubbed into a long shot.

When adapting a novel do you work much with the original author?

No, we much prefer not to meet him at all. Once the film rights are sold the book is going into another realm. The problems are so different that we may never go back to the book once we've read it. The author rarely, if ever, has rights of approval on the script. Obviously the point of a book must be preserved (though there are notorious cases when it has not been), but apart from this the screenwriter *must* have his hands entirely free.

Bernard Shaw said that the original author of a novel should prepare his own script and, ideally, turn himself into a director and direct it.

In that case, he shouldn't write a novel to begin with, he should write a film script. Nowadays there are quite a number of novels published which are obviously film scripts in embryo, written with the intention that they should be turned into screenplays with a minimum of alteration. Even so, it is rarely the original author who prepares the script.

When the director is other than one of yourselves, do you work very closely with him?

As closely as possible. A good relationship is essential but unfortunately rarely sustained throughout because so often the writer is away working on something else. To a certain extent you are also involved with the art director and cameraman because in the early stages you are the only person who is 'see-ing' the film. It is useful too to visit all locations. In *Hannibal Brooks* (1968, directed by Michael Winner) we went to Austria with the director before we had written a word, and this was invaluable because the mere fact of seeing the locations sug-gested all sorts of additional points which were not in the book.

3. The Director

'Film is the director's medium' may seem a truism nowadays, but this has not always been the case. At one period, especially in America when, as Fred Zinnemann puts it, films were being made on the assembly line, the director was very often just an employee of the studio – an important employee, but an employee just the same – given a script with all the necessary instructions marked on it in readiness, and told to shoot it as indicated. His work was then taken from him and edited, amended, sometimes even partly re-shot, by other hands.

Nowadays the director is almost invariably the paramount figure in the production of the feature film. There are producers who take over a large part of the creative work in their own project, engaging a director and sometimes even dismissing him as soon as shooting is finished; but in general the director is able to keep, and insists on keeping, the closest control over all aspects of the picture, from the preliminary script to the final cut.

To define the job of the director in broad terms is simple – to determine its limits is virtually impossible: his is the ultimate responsibility for the entire artistic side of the production. Though obviously he consults and delegates, in normal circumstances he has the overall vision and the final word. In 1933,

Ernst Lubitsch commented in a way that is equally relevant today on a difficulty which faces any feature film director:

'What so many people forget when they criticize the work of a film director is that he has to cater for varying tastes, all over the world. When a play is produced on the New York stage, for instance, the producer can stress certain points, introduce definite "business" which he knows will appeal to the New York audience. If he were to produce the same play in London, he might change his method drastically, because he knows that London would appreciate certain situations that a New York audience would miss; and vice versa. Imagine, then, the enormous difficulties that face a film-maker. He has to produce a screenplay that will appeal not only to New York and London, but also to the Middle West of America, the Irish and Scottish peasants, the Australian sheep farmer and the South African businessman. This will give you some idea of the difficulties with which a film director has to contend and why so much time and thought are necessary if a worldwide reputation is to be secured.'[1]

The position is frequently complicated by the fact that the director may also be the producer, the leading actor, the writer or cameraman of his film, and will often control the cutting process so firmly that he could be said to be the chief editor as well: Chaplin, Hitchcock, Welles are famous examples. In recent years directors have tended more and more to combine one or more auxiliary activities with the job of directing.

The Assistant Director might be described as a sort of 'set foreman': he is responsible for overseeing all the practical on-set activities. It is his job to see that all actors are ready 'on call', to handle the crowd and small-part players, prepare the daily callsheet, maintain discipline, smooth ruffled tempers, generally ensure the efficient running of each day's shooting – a job, in fact, requiring tact, patience, authority, good humour, mental alacrity, physical stamina, vocal power, and the ability to combine the qualities of sergeant-major and father confessor.

1. Quoted by Herman G. Weinberg in *The Lubitsch Touch*, E. P. Dutton, New York, 1968.

The interviews that follow give some indication of the power, responsibility and involvement of present-day directors and of the parallels and divergencies of their approach to the multiple problems encountered in the making of feature films.

John Frankenheimer

John Frankenheimer (U.S.A.) was born in 1930 and formerly worked in television. He has directed the following films: *The Young Stranger* (1957); *The Young Savages* (1961); *All Fall Down* (1961); *The Manchurian Candidate* (1962); *Birdman of Alcatraz* (1962); *Seven Days in May* (1964); *The Train* (1964); *Seconds* (1966); *Grand Prix* (1967); *The Extraordinary Seaman* (1968); *Gypsy Moths* (1968); *The Fixer* (1968).

'There are four integral parts of film-making: scripting, casting, shooting and editing. Each is equally important, but if I were to be told I could only control three, I would give up the shooting. If you send someone out and he shoots enough material, provided you have a good script, have cast well, and have final editing privilege I think you can turn it into a film. In the three most important elements – scripting, casting and editing – my early experience on 125 live television shows was invaluable. To start with, it was an exercise in cutting. The television director has the final cut on the air, because it is his choice that the public sees. The shooting technique may differ from movies, but basically they both employ a camera. If you have a good eye and learn to use a camera on television, it is a simple change to filming. You don't take so many close-ups and have a broader canvas, but there's not much difference otherwise. I like, for instance, to use a wide-angle lens fairly frequently in my films, and I learnt this almost entirely from television.'

You are now an independent director?

No director is fully independent, if only because he has to get financial backing. I have an associate, Edward Lewis, who is an equal partner in my films, and I have made my last seven pictures with him as producer. Our decisions are joint ones. We are independent in that we have final cut, and are not interfered with provided we don't go way over our budget. But there is also the question of the stars to consider. People sometimes say the star system is dead, but this is just not true. Film stars are being paid more now, and have more influence, than ever in their lives. If the movie star is dead, I'd like to be dead that way!

Do you work very closely with the scriptwriter?

It's almost a collaboration, though I am not a writer – I don't compose the actual dialogue. Any director is in a sense part author of his film, for the simple reason that he decides what is going to be on the screen, and where and when.

Do you use a very detailed script?

If it's going to be a complicated action scene, yes. Take the sequence in *The Train* where the Spitfire comes down over it, almost scraping the top of the engine. This was an extremely difficult scene to do, because you had one object travelling at 35 m.p.h. and another at 300 m.p.h. and you had to achieve a sense of movement between the two, and keep it clear as to what was happening. It was much more difficult, for instance, than anything in *Grand Prix* where we were concerned with objects moving at the same speed. Every moment of *The Train* sequence was worked out in advance, and went fine until we began to shoot it, but when we saw the first rushes they were unusable because I'd put on much too wide-angled a lens – the plane was past you before you could see it. So we had to re-shoot with long-focal lenses. The sequence took nearly three weeks to shoot. In *Grand Prix* the problem was to make each race seem different. I was not wholly successful, but everything was planned beforehand – each specific shot.

With a straightforward scene between actors in a room, however, I will not have many preconceived ideas, but improvise and rehearse a lot. Actors should have a large share in deciding what they are going to do and how they are going to do it. They should be treated as creative artists, not as puppets.

Do you generally use many cameras?

Film is a cheap commodity in terms of picture-making, and I use a lot of it. For action scenes I'll employ as many cameras as I can get. And often enough I'm thankful I did so. Take *The*

Train again, the scene where it runs off the rails, finishing with the shot of the revolving wheel in the foreground. This shot, which everyone praised, was a complete accident. It was to be a routine derailment, and we had eight cameras on hand. I lined up seven of them, and forgot the eighth. Just as we were about to go the French cameraman came up to me and said: 'What would you like me to do with zis camera?' By this time I was feeling pretty frustrated and I said: 'Go over there and bury it!' 'Bury it?' he asked. 'Yes, bury it!' He went off looking a bit bewildered. Well, we shot the scene. The train came along – but the stuntman working the accident panicked and pulled the train lever much too far. We saw the train, at 20 m.p.h. coming right at us. Everyone ran. The train came off the track and wiped out all seven cameras. The only remaining camera was the one which the little Frenchman had buried in the ground, and that was the shot you saw.

In *Grand Prix*, photographing cars going at speeds up to 120 m.p.h. in Monte Carlo, we used twenty cameras and were glad of it, because out of those twenty we only got good shots from six or seven.

When a director starts his career and wants to impress the crews and everyone else, he likes to take a scene in one great big shot and say: 'Well, that's finished, let's move on,' so that everyone else says, 'My God, he's a genius!' As you get a bit more experience you still try to do this, but you cover yourself by shooting close-ups of all the actors concerned in the scene. When you are eventually alone in the cutting-room, and all the actors are away making other films and the crew off somewhere else, and you want to cut out one line of dialogue, and you can't do it because you haven't shot any covering material – that's when you learn what you need to have.

Do you prefer location or studio working conditions?

I prefer location, but if you have to film scenes in a small, cramped room it's more convenient to work in a studio, where you can move walls and so on if necessary – and once you've worked a lot on location, and know what you're doing, then it's all right to be able to move walls. If a director is not used to using his camera in a real room, however, he is apt to take out a wall and put the camera somewhere it couldn't possibly be – for example the classic shot through the bookcase. *I don't think you should ever put the camera somewhere you can't go yourself*, such as happens when a love scene is photographed behind flickering flames. I have never been in a fireplace! If a camera comes through a ship's porthole into a cabin, you know at once that you're on a set. But of course this doesn't always apply, it depends entirely on the subject. Stanley Kubrick could not possibly have shot *2001: A Space Odyssey* on location!

You make a good deal of use of the hand-held camera. What are your feelings about this?

It can be very effective and convenient, but is often greatly overdone. The French directors have the logical explanation of it. They said: 'When we started out, we would have loved to have had all the lovely complicated dollies and rails, but we simply didn't have the money for them. So we *had* to use a bicycle and a hand-held camera.' In other words, they made a virtue of necessity. I think it is good for newsreel or documentary-type effects, and it is true that an audience should sometimes be made aware of the presence of a camera – which they always are when it is hand-held. But the idea that this is the way people really see things is nonsense. You don't see the whole room wobbling violently when you walk across it. The human eye has a self-levelling mechanism that makes a perfect dolly out of the body.

How do you feel about the apparent gradual disappearance of the black-and-white film?

The first colour film I made was *Grand Prix*, because the only way you could tell the difference between the racing cars was by distinguishing the red from the green. Looking back over the other movies I've made, I don't think any of them would have been improved by colour. However, like many things which start off for the wrong reason (e.g. television), some good is coming out of colour as film stock and lighting equipment improve and we gradually learn how to use it more effectively.

Do you often find that subtleties and hidden meanings which you never intended are read into your films by critics?

The classic example was in *The Manchurian Candidate*, where the man is shot and milk comes from his body instead of blood. The real explanation is very simple and prosaic. My problem in that picture was the same as that which faces the director of *Hamlet* – both contain an awful lot of corpses. I had seven to deal with, and the difficulty was to make the killings different, to prevent it all from becoming monotonous. So I thought, why not shoot the old boy through the milk container he's carrying? So we did – and got credited with all sorts of symbolic overtones we'd never even thought about.

Sidney Lumet

Sidney Lumet (U.S.A.) was born in 1924. He was a child actor, and later became a television producer. He has directed *Twelve Angry Men* (1957); *Stage Struck* (1958); *That Kind of Woman* (1959); *The Fugitive Kind* (1960); *A View from the Bridge* (1961); *Long Day's Journey into Night* (1962); *Fail Safe* (1964); *The Pawnbroker* (1965); *The Hill* (1965); *The Group* (1965); *The Deadly Affair* (1966); *Bye Bye Braverman* (1967); *The Appointment* (1969); *The Seagull* (1969).

'The advantage for a director of previous training in television is that in a live transmission you are, so to speak, editing as you go, so that the technique becomes almost automatic. This ability to select what is important dramatically in advance eventually becomes a very economic way of making movies. Another advantage is that the laws of optics are constant: a 35 mm. lens does the same thing on a TV camera, a motion picture camera and a still camera. The visual training you receive is irreplaceable, because it can only be obtained by sheer exposure of the eye to what the various lenses can do. The disadvantage is the difference of scale: transferring from television to movies you lose awareness of the enormous division between the 21-inch and the 50-foot image.'

Do you work very closely with the scriptwriter?

It varies very much. On *The Pawnbroker*, where I felt the original script was too sentimental, taking the easy way out, I did a great deal of work, and in some instances where even the rewrite was not satisfactory I improvised scenes. In other cases I have done nothing – the script arrived in what I felt was almost perfect shape – for example *Bye Bye Braverman* and *The Group*, both of which I left entirely unchanged.

I have never adjusted a script to fit a particular star. I cast in relation to what is written, since it is that which attracted me in the first place. The player, leading or not, must fit in with what we have set out to do.

If a script is given to me containing indications of camera angles or stage directions I rarely use them. I find that most writers are not directors, just as most directors are not writers. There have been cases where a writer makes suggestions as to how he wants a scene handled which contain a lot of sense, and then I have followed them – but they are definitely in a minority.

Do you improvise much?

Again, it varies. There are some scripts in which I feel the language is so vital that no freedom at all is permissible. *The Seagull* is an obvious example – nothing must be changed. On the other hand, improvisation can add tremendous value to a scene. In *The Pawnbroker*, the scene between the shop boy and his mother talking together in Spanish while he has his bath was totally improvised on the set during shooting: other sequences in the same film were similarly handled. Sometimes during rehearsal we may improvise for a whole day, subsequently building up the scene from the dialogue which grew up during this impromptu performance. Generally, as far as the actor is concerned in this respect, I would say that he is living under a benevolent dictatorship – having tremendous freedom within a confined range!

Do you rehearse a good deal before going on the set?

Enormously. I need it for myself, to find if I am on the right track, and I also think that the actor benefits. The security it brings him liberates him, so that he can be prepared for the best possible accident during shooting, because all other worries have been eliminated – such as where he is going, what it is all about, where any particular scene lies in the entire 'arc' of the character. Once an actor finds himself standing on a structurally solidly built part, in the acting sense, it's amazing how loose and free he will become.

Do you prefer to work on location or in the studio?

Almost always location. Art is not reality, art is truth, and if one is searching for truth one must at least begin with reality. It seems to me that most studio exteriors are the very negation of reality. With interiors, it's a matter of choice. In *The Appointment* I shot all the interiors on location. I found that the reality gained visually was lost because the sound was so poor I had to go into the looping (post-synching) studio: 90 per cent of the picture was looped, which I think has hurt it. It's a question of balance – does the visual reality of the real rooms compensate for the vocal loss?

Do you like to use multi-camera technique?

It may be a hangover from television, but I love this technique. I think the old Hollywood precept that once you shift the angle fifteen degrees you cannot light it properly is sheer nonsense. Apart from the fact that my cameramen have always lit my multi-camera set-ups perfectly, with no loss of quality, there are often instances where the overall is so much more important. In *The Seagull*, many scenes between Vanessa Redgrave and David Warner were shot with two cameras because this preserved the unity of performance between two players of extreme emotional intensity. I knew that whatever happened on any take would happen between both of them – they would fly together and fall together.

Do you use many takes?

I find that if I have to go beyond four takes it means either that I have directed wrongly, or that the actor is 'off' in some way. With almost every actor of major talent – Marlon Brando, Vanessa Redgrave, Lee Cobb, Simone Signoret, Katherine Hepburn, James Mason – we get it early, or we've made a mistake somewhere. On *The Seagull*, which is a very long film, I used very little footage, 85,000 feet *exposed* – on *Twelve Angry Men*, 63,000. You're better off rehearsing the moves, mechanically in the case of difficult scenes, until everybody is absolutely secure, and keeping the actors from going full out until the take – then get it early.

Do you control the editing closely?

So closely that you might say my hand never leaves the brake of the moviola. Every frame counts. The moment of a cut, the moment you physically slice the film, is as critical to the picture as the choice of lens, the lens opening, the placement of key lighting – too critical to be left to another mind. If a cut were changed in a movie of mine I think I would take my name off it; it's that important to me.

Do you like the use of hand-held cameras?

They have tremendous advantages if used in specific ways, in solving technical – or emotional – problems. In *The Hill*, the scene where Alfie Lynch is running up and down the hill, at one moment the operator was actually carried by two grips. Overuse can weaken the impact fatally – and always one should be aware of that 50-foot scale. The violence of a jiggling frame blown up to fifty feet is too often forgotten when rushes are being viewed on a small screen. There have been instances where I have shot a whole sequence which everybody afterwards thought was done with a hand-held camera – for example the last twelve minutes of *The Pawnbroker*, from the moment of the attack on the shop. This was in fact photographed by three cameras simultaneously, none of them hand-held, and was shot only once. The improvisational feel had nothing to do with the hand camera.

Do you use second unit at all?

Never. If I don't shoot it, it's not going to be in the picture! In a form which requires such an enormous number of people (even on a small set there will be eight of them trying to do the creative work of one) it seems to me that the matter of channelling the control through one source is so critical that any time you let it out of your hands you are dissipating the total artistic effect. There are, of course, obvious exceptions to this – Andrew Marton's wonderful chariot race in *Ben Hur*, for instance.

Do you regret the present prevalence of colour over black-and-white?

In my view there's really no point in thinking of or hoping for any reversion to black-and-white. We must just put it out of our minds. In any case I think that as directors we have all been brainwashed by the idea that colour can't be as effective as black-and-white because we'd always been used to the latter, and because the early colour films we saw were so garish and tasteless that it ruined us for taking them seriously. Now that we have no choice we have really gone to work on the problems and I consider that we're beginning to solve them. In *The Deadly Affair*, Freddie Young and I worked out a system, I think used here for the first time, of pre-fogging the actual stock, the negative, beforehand in order to damp the colour down: the result was, in my opinion, a dramatic value added to the film. Conversely, in *The Appointment*, Carlo de Parma and I set as our objective not only *not* to mute the colour, but to make very heavy use of it. In *The Seagull*, Gerry Fisher removed the 85 filter used on exteriors and substituted two others which he himself designed. This resulted in a brilliant utilization of the blues in the first act, and of the greens, the yellows, and the sunlight itself in the second act – contributing something to *The Seagull* by fighting *for* the colour in the healthiest way. I don't think that I would again try to mute colour, to reduce it as closely as possible to black-and-white. Beginning with the work of the art director, and progressing through the camera in the lighting, the lens opening, the use of filters, my aim is to try to utilize colour as another and powerful dramatic tool.

Do you particularly enjoy that part of a director's job which is immediately concerned with the actors?

Working closely with actors is one of the prime joys of directing. After all, the revelation of human behaviour finally comes down to the human being. They are the heart of the movie. There are directors who try to reveal it in other ways, but to me it is always ultimately through the performance of the actor. Take the moment, for instance, in *The Deadly Affair* when James Mason, seated in the theatre, suddenly realizes that the man who has betrayed him on an espionage level is also the man who is betraying him with his wife; and all of a sudden he has to vomit: Mason's look, the way his hand comes up to his mouth, the way his body reacts as he runs from his seat to the men's room. It seems to me that a director who cannot stimulate that level of performance has lost one of his most valuable tools.

Do you like to combine the jobs of producer and director?

Producing is a bore. One doesn't particularly enjoy negotiating with agents for actors, and personally I absolutely detest the business of selling the completed picture, meeting advertising and sales departments, fighting for a theatre, etc. I do it, and I think most directors do it, for one very simple reason: there are fewer good producers than any other profession connected with movies. Thus I would rather undertake the job myself than have to argue with someone who thinks he is another creative force in the picture. It is another of those dissipating factors I referred to earlier. There are of course genuinely creative producers – such as Kenneth Hyman who worked with me on *The Hill*, and Marty Paul on *The Appointment* – who do not let the areas overlap. They are there with casting suggestions or script suggestions, but in no instance is it anything but good healthy discussion, with no attempts to impose their point of view on the picture. And in addition they fight for the film when it is completed. But most producers are more of a problem than a contribution, and so it becomes easier to produce it yourself. The man who says 'Print!' is the man with the primary responsibility in a movie – and that is the director.

Jack Clayton

Jack Clayton (Britain) was born in 1921. Before becoming a director, he worked as assistant director, production manager and producer. He has directed *Room at the Top* (1960–61); *The Innocents* (1962–3); *The Pumpkin Eater* (1967); *Our Mother's House* (1968).

'Not so long ago, the director was an employee of a studio. He was given a script, went on the set, suggested what the actors and camera should do, and, when the shooting was over, put on his hat and went home, leaving his producer and editor to finish the job. These days, things are different. For example, I am fortunate enough to be my own producer and so am involved even before the property is bought. Then I work closely on the script with the writer from the first draft and, by the same token, with the editor right through to the final married print. Today, when a distributor or film company backs a project, the choice of director is given as much importance as that of the star. Indeed, while technically the distributor has the final say as regards casting the star or stars, he rarely turns down a director's suggestion. And the director has another unseen influence too, because most stars today want to know who the director will be before accepting the part. But I often wonder why it should be expected that the *public* should care who directs the film they go to see.'

Do you work from a very detailed script?

Personally, I don't like to be handed a script complete with camera angles and so on: 'Cut from the scream to the train-whistle.' I much prefer a series of uncluttered scenes conveying the required ideas and dialogue. In any case, most really good writers themselves prefer not to be hampered by technicalities. For me, as the director, it's not a question of 'How do I shoot this scene?' but 'Out of seven hundred ways I *could* shoot this scene, which is best?' That's what the job is about.

Do you rehearse a great deal?

No, not really. While I do make so-called 'last-minute' changes quite often, I'd say that less than 50 per cent of my shooting is actually improvised on the set. Of course, one of the main advantages of working with the writer from an early stage is that the point of the scene has already been evolved, so one has a pre-vision of how it should be shot. I also try to adapt my method of direction to the individual actor – to find a way in which I can influence, rather than 'direct' him or her. In this way, the actor is allowed a certain freedom of expression which he enjoys and which, I think, contributes to his performance.

Do you overshoot a lot?

I generally go to quite a number of takes, especially on a film like *Our Mother's House*, where I'm directing children. As you know, footage is the cheapest commodity in the film-making process, so my view is: have your second thoughts on the floor and shoot then whatever you think you may need later in the editing stage. After all, you can't cut a good suit with insufficient cloth.

Do you prefer to work in black-and-white or colour?

I'm a total fan of black-and-white and I think it will come back in a few years' time. Of course, colour can be used for dramatic or atmospheric effect, but I think it's wrong that you should be virtually compelled to use it whether the subject calls for it or not. From the director's point of view, too, colour can present a pretty frightening problem when it comes to processing. It doesn't matter how good the laboratory, the print the conveyor-belt churns out never seems to match up to the one you fed into it. *Our Mother's House* was my first colour film. I spent six weeks on it in the labs, and the lab technicians turned somersaults in their efforts to help. Between us, we got the best results we could – but the final print still lacked the quality of the original 'rushes'. This was especially the case in the outdoor scenes, which incidentally taught me a lesson: never shoot exteriors in bright sunshine – they'll come out looking like garish picture postcards.

How do you feel about the new 'freedom of technique'?

I think a lot of camera gimmickry derives from television, where it may sometimes be necessary, but is, I suspect, frequently overdone. It's the director's job to tell his story in the best and simplest way he can, and his technique is most effective when concealed. If it shows, if it becomes noticeable, then it must surely detract from the audience's involvement.

You have a great affection for the zoom lens?

That's true. But not really because of its normally accepted function of allowing one to zoom in or out at speed for dramatic effect – although I did find it useful in this way in *The Innocents*. It was while shooting tests for *The Pumpkin Eater* that I had the chance of exploring its other capabilities – and in fact I ended up by using it for nearly a third of the picture. With a multi-focal lens the zoom can be used like a camera on tracks, only far more discreetly. So much so that it need – and should – never be noticeable. For example, in *Our Mother's House* the children never knew when they were being singled out for close-ups: as far as they were concerned, the camera was miles away. And in this film, too, the zoom was invaluable for another, very practical reason. Almost all the scenes took place in an actual Victorian-style house in Croydon – and it meant we didn't need to make any major structural alterations to provide camera space, nor did we have to 'cheat'. Using a normal camera dolly in such a confined space would have been impossible – yet without freedom of movement the results would have had to be horribly static. So if it hadn't been for the zoom, we'd have been in real trouble. Of course, it's a tricky thing to handle and needs brilliant camera boys – especially when used in this way – but I don't think it can be surpassed for obtaining a fluid, unobtrusive, continuous movement within the frame.

Do you sometimes find yourself credited by critics with brilliant touches which were really quite unintentional?

Occasionally. For example, in *The Pumpkin Eater* we had a shot of the woman lying in bed smoking and talking to her first husband. It started with the camera focused on a cigarette in her hand, then panned away across the room to a photograph on the piano. But when we ran the final scene – which was all in one shot – it just didn't seem right. With one continuous shot, when it doesn't work what the hell can you do? Then suddenly I had an idea: why not play the whole scene in reverse? *Start* on the photograph and then move round the room, finishing on the woman smoking in bed. The only problem was, of course, that when we got to her the smoke was going back *into* the cigarette. 'Oh well,' we said, 'perhaps no one will notice.' But they did. Several of the critics complimented me on my clever use of sexual symbolism!

Lindsay Anderson

Lindsay Anderson (Britain) was born in 1923. He was the co-founder and editor of the film review *Sequence*, and he has directed a number of documentaries, including *Thursday's Children*, which won a Hollywood Academy Award in 1955. His feature films are: *This Sporting Life* (1963); *The White Bus* (1967); *If ...* (1969).

'I think that film at its best – or at any rate at its most poetic – is the personal expression of one man. This is not to decry the many other methods of film-making, whether for entertainment or instruction, but I feel that, as director, when you are making a feature film with some sixty people around you all the time you must try to preserve a sense of independence and freedom at its creative centre. I am by nature extremely subjective, and instinctively identify myself very closely with my work at every stage. I find it very difficult to detach myself from the film when it is finished, and watch it turned into a piece of merchandise. I even worry when it is on release because I can't supervise the prints which the audience will be seeing; perhaps with reason, because the whole state of film reproduction is surprisingly little known to anyone outside the industry – critics remark on the poor quality of colour systems without realizing that laboratory standards are so low that if 100 prints are struck, 90 of them will probably be bad. But of course personal supervision to this extent is impossible without either collapsing or going mad!'

Do you meet with much pressure from distributors in regard to subject and other points?

Of course original subjects are always difficult to get finance for – particularly if you want to make a film without stars. But once you have got your backing, and if you've got it honestly, then you should be able to make the film on your own terms. Sometimes eyebrows will be raised, or there might be a tendency to panic when the completed film is run, but if you stick firmly and courteously to your guns – and if you really know what you are talking about – ninety-nine times out of a hundred you get away with it.

Do you like to work from a detailed script and adhere closely to it, or do you improvise a great deal?

The scripts I've worked on are very simple and direct in expression, without a lot of adjectives. Many scripts sent to me from distributors are quite unreadable, rather like bad novels. I have been involved in the writing of every one of my scripts, and like to have them as a very strong lifeline, very well prepared structurally, but I will then improvise the method of shooting. Working with actors is a very delicate and intimate process. A director must always remember that he has been responsible for choosing them in the first place, so that implicit in his choice must be the intuition that they are right for the various characters and have something to contribute in their approach to them. I never try to impose my ideas on them, but to arrive at the final result by collaboration rather than dictatorship. To that extent I am always prepared to move away from the original script.

Do you like to have plenty of rehearsal time?

We rehearsed *This Sporting Life* for two whole weeks before going on the floor, working straight through the script as in the theatre. This is necessary if the basis of the film is a complex developing character situation, because the scenes can so rarely be shot in script order. It gives the actor an idea of the total scheme, the graph of his role, so that having got the conception in his mind as a whole he can then jump to and fro in time during shooting.

Do you prefer location or studio work?

If you're shooting dramatic material the kind of privacy and manoeuvrability you get in a studio is a great advantage. I should not like to have had to film *This Sporting Life*, with its extended dramatic scenes, on location. The world is on top of you on location, and this can often make it very difficult for the actors. But there is one very great advantage in working on location, which is that you engage your own unit, and can handpick them yourself. There are a number of small studios into which you can take your own technicians, merely hiring the building (as we did for the small interiors in *If . . .*), but if you go into one of the major studios, you have to use their staff. This can be an extremely important consideration. In the end, however, the question is generally answered for you by the matter of expense, which on location can be very great.

Have you any preference between colour and black-and-white? Was there a symbolic plan behind your apparently arbitrary combination of colour and monochrome in If . . .?

The first question is really an academic one nowadays – you just accept that you have to shoot in colour, because of the eventual possibility of sale to television.

Originally I did not think of colour in relation to *If . . .*, but when we found we had to use it my cameraman Miroslav Ondricek came over from Prague and we went to Cheltenham to look at the chapel, which was very large, with big windows where the light was constantly changing. He said that in the two days which was all the schedule allowed he couldn't shoot such an immense area in colour, and also compensate for changing weather conditions, with the small amount of artificial light available. We experimented with a new and very fast stock, but the quality was not good enough, so we decided to do it in black-and-white. Thus the immediate reason was a purely practical one. However, I had of course other feelings about it as well. Ondricek and I had already mixed colour and black-and-white sequences in *The White Bus*, though in reverse proportion, and on looking back I realized that I had liked the idea of varying the surface of the film. Some people, particularly critics, who are always more selfconscious than ordinary audiences, tried at first to attach symbolic significance to the colour changes in *If . . .*, and it worried them. I think, however, that you see the colour with new eyes when it follows a short spell of monochrome. In a film of unbroken colour you are apt to 'lose' it after about half an hour, and I think the variation causes the whole surface of the film to become much more expressive. Also, in the case of *If . . .*, we had a film which progressed from naturalism to fantasy: I didn't want any tricks or devices to signal degrees of reality, and I felt that by varying the surface in this way I prepared the audience for a film which was not a strictly naturalistic narrative picture. It also deliberately served to jerk them back into the consciousness that they were watching a film: as indicated in the quotation at the start of *If . . .*, I was anxious that they should be on the alert, using their heads, rather than sinking back into a warm bath of emotion.

Do you find directing in the theatre more artistically satisfying than in the cinema?

The media are so different that it's difficult to compare them in this way. A film *belongs* to its director in a way that a play does not, but the pleasure of working in the theatre is the pleasure of working with people. Directing a film is a much lonelier business. I can hardly talk about it as a pleasure, because it's such a struggle – one is forever conscious of time running out, money being spent every moment of the day. It's a continuous state of tension. But of course in the end you're left with something that will last.

John Huston

John Huston (U.S.A.) was born in 1906, the son of Walter Huston, and began his career in Hollywood as a screenwriter. He has directed the following films: *The Maltese Falcon* (1941); *In This Our Life* (1942); *Across the Pacific* (1943); *The Treasure of the Sierra Madre* (1948); *Key Largo* (1948); *We Were Strangers* (1949); *The Asphalt Jungle* (1950); *The Red Badge of Courage* (1951); *The African Queen* (1952); *Moulin Rouge* (1953); *Beat the Devil* (1954); *Moby Dick* (1956); *Heaven Knows, Mr Allison* (1957); *The Barbarian and the Geisha* (1958); *The Roots of Heaven* (1958); *The Unforgiven* (1960); *The Misfits* (1961); *Freud* (1962); *The List of Adrian Messenger* (1963); *The Night of the Iguana* (1964); *The Bible* (1966); (first part of) *Casino Royale* (1967); *Reflections in a Golden Eye* (1967); *Sinful Davey* (1969); *The Kremlin Letter* (1970).

'I work very closely on the scripts of my films. Long before shooting begins, the script is completed in detail. And then during the filming, as new ideas occur, there is more writing to be done on the script from day to day. Making motion pictures is merely an extension of writing. I prefer to work from a finished screenplay. But you don't always pay attention to the camera instructions even if you've written them yourself. So far as the dialogue is concerned I prefer to stay as close to the script as possible.'

Your films have covered a wide range of subjects – is there any particular aspect of a script as a whole which attracts you to make a film of it?

Not that I'm aware of. My choice of subjects is only governed by the interest the material arouses in me.

Do you rehearse much before going on the floor?

Hardly ever. And once we are on the floor, the camera positions have been worked out and the set is lit, I sometimes even shoot rehearsals.

Do you think it is a great advantage to shoot in strict chron- ology – as in The Misfits *– whenever possible?*

Yes. I certainly prefer to shoot in continuity and manage to do so most of the time. Any director must prefer to do so for obvious reasons. For example, suppose we are shooting out of continuity and we have a man with a bruise on the right side of his face. At a later moment we have to shoot a fight scene which naturally occurs earlier in the story. Now we must arrange to have the blow delivered in such a way that it will account cred- ibly for the bruise. Shooting in continuity is sometimes incon- venient but in most cases it offers more advantages than shooting out of continuity.

Do you find that acting in your own films – playing under your own direction, so to speak, presents any special prob- lems?

First I must operate as a director. By using a stand-in I get the set-up for the scene. Then I step in and make it. Sometimes I find myself the actor doing things only the director should be doing, such as watching the camera operator or the boom man. Of course, this doesn't do my performance any good, so I shoot the scene again. I suppose I give myself more takes than I do any of my other actors.

Do you prefer location work, or the more controlled studio conditions?

This depends largely on the subject matter, but I suppose I incline towards location work. Despite the fact that there are always more difficulties when filming on location, the locations themselves are very often a source of inspiration.

Do you keep a close hand on the editing?

Very close. I begin editing as the rushes come in and this continues throughout the filming. In this way, a few weeks after the picture has been filmed I've got a fairly good cut. After this first cut I leave the picture in the hands of the editor for a few weeks. He is then able to try out some of his own ideas. This usually takes him from three weeks to a month. Then I view the film again and make additional alterations until finally I'm run- ning every other hour, with the corrections being made be- tween screenings. After ten days to two weeks of this the picture is ready to be measured so that the composer can start writing.

Are you happy with the almost universal use of colour, or do you still wish you could sometimes make a black-and-white movie?

When you have a psychological story to tell, sometimes colour gets between you and the story. Your eye deflects on it, as it were. It is as absurd to say that everything should be done in colour as it would be to deny black-and-white as a medium to an artist. *Guernica* is probably Picasso's greatest painting. As with other devices, I deplore the use of colour simply for colour's sake. Of course, many pictures do require colour – but not simply *per se*. Ideally every subject should have a different colour solution.

Apart from the classic case of The Red Badge of Courage, *have you suffered a lot from distortions of your work by distributors or producers – the withdrawal of the special colour version of* Reflections in a Golden Eye, *for instance?*

Yes, in some other instances I've been properly bitched. *The Barbarian and the Geisha* as seen by the public was not the picture I made. Nor for that matter is the more recent *Sinful Davey.*

Do you think it advantageous for a director to be his own producer?

I welcome the presence of the producer, but not on the set necessarily. (As a rule the better the producer, the less he frequents the set.) The producer takes a great deal of the load off the director's back and there should be no infringement of the prerogatives of one by the other. The producer's concern is to work out the logistics and to see that the money goes where it should. I would much rather have no producer than one not highly competent. On the other hand, I'm very grateful to the producer who can allow me to give my entire attention to the shooting of scenes, to the making of the picture itself.

How would you compare working conditions in England, America and Italy?

Today working conditions in films are more or less equal all round the world, even here in Ireland where a picture industry is in the process of emerging. I'm rather reluctant to make a picture in England because of some labour restrictions which in my experience seem unwise. These restrictions, in my judgement, offer less protection to the workers than they offer obstacles to the directors. This isn't to say that an English crew isn't as good technically as any crew in the world. Wherever I find myself making pictures I invariably have some British technicians, simply because of their excellence. Moreover, studios around the world are about the same these days. Of course, the most recently built studios would naturally offer some technical advantages. The De Laurentiis studios in Italy are the most recently built big studios and therefore have the most modern facilities. This explains why three of my recent films have been made there.

What do you think of the prospects for young directors today – and what is the greatest asset, or ability, for them to have?

The successes that new directors are having would seem to indicate that their prospects have seldom been brighter. Before I made my first picture my producer Henry Blanke gave me this piece of advice: 'You should think of each shot as you make it as the most important one in the film.' I pass this on. Ability to concentrate all of his powers of attention at a given moment is perhaps the greatest asset a picture-maker can have.

George Sidney

George Sidney (U.S.A.) was born in 1911. Before directing screen musicals he was a musician and director of shorts. He has directed *Free and Easy* (1941); *Pacific Rendezvous* (1942); *Thousands Cheer* (1943); *Bathing Beauty* (1944); *Anchors Aweigh* (1945); *The Harvey Girls* (1946); *Holiday in Mexico* (1946); *Cass Timburlane* (1947); *The Three Musketeers* (1948); *The Red Danube* (1949); *Annie Get Your Gun* (1950); *Key to the City* (1950); *Show Boat* (1951); *Scaramouche* (1952); *Kiss Me, Kate* (1953); *Jupiter's Darling* (1955); *The Eddie Duchin Story* (1956); *Jeanne Eagels* (1957); *Pal Joey* (1957); *Who Was That Lady?* (1960); *Pepe* (1960); *Bye Bye Birdie* (1963); *The Swinger* (1966); *Half a Sixpence* (1967).

'To make a screen musical without complete musical and technical knowledge would be, to me, the same as a surgeon operating without knowledge of anatomy. I have studied music in all forms, including composition, harmony, arranging, theory, conducting, history, as well as learning to play (not well) four instruments. I'm a minor composer and a member of ASCAP. In fact, there's no facet of music I have left unexplored, and I'm a constant experimenter, with elaborate recording and re-recording equipment both in my office and in my home.'

Have you composed the music for any of your own films?

I wouldn't be that presumptuous, when I've been fortunate enough to have been associated with men of music like Irving Berlin, Cole Porter, Rogers and Hart, André Previn, Tchaikovsky, Shostakovich, Beethoven, Rachmaninov. But I take a very active part in editing the music, and work directly with the arrangers and the musical supervisor.

What do you find are the special problems of filming musicals?

They are mostly in bringing stage material to the screen. It's a job of construction. Stage musicals are mostly in a two-act format. Usually the story is basically in the first act. This has to be balanced into a cinematic pattern that gives the story and the music a cohesive presentation. Sometimes it is necessary to drop numbers and add a new one – the originals just don't work. Some purists always say: 'It's not as it was on the stage' – and right they are. It is not a photographed stage play, but a film. All material must be adapted for the screen. Selection and creative blending is essential.

Do you come on the set with a very complete script?

In musicals you plan way ahead. I have story boards made (photographic or sketched) even in advance of the musical arrangements. This is essential, so that ultimately there is a complete marriage of sight and sound, music and choreography. This doesn't just happen by chance. All must be minutely planned in advance. The director has the ultimate vision. He must work individually and collectively with the composer, the conductor, the choreographer, the arranger, vocal specialists, art director, music and film editor, costumier, photographer, recorder, artists and all technicians.

Do you use second units at all?

No. Two men, no matter how good, cannot have the same inner vision. It has been done, but the audience has suffered, as they felt they were witnessing two different films, but did not know why.

What about the editing of a musical?

The viewer should never know where a cut is. It must all appear as a happening. The cutting takes place before you shoot the film, it is not just thousands of miles of film that you put together like a jigsaw puzzle. Every cut must be planned for rhythm and flow for ear and eye. There are rules you don't violate – like not cutting in the middle of a phrase, or in the middle of a musical figure. You keep the bar chart and music with you whilst shooting. This becomes your musical script. Your cutting notes follow you on the bar chart to the cutting-room. This, again, is where you must have a working knowledge of music – be able to read music and orchestration, and know where or where not to cut in relation to key changes, tempo and rhythm pattern.

During your period of directing musicals you must have encountered great changes in technique?

The musical has had a complete metamorphosis. When I started, we were making musicals by the pound – thousands of legs kicking, thousands of trombones blaring, and breath-taking overhead shots. This we grew out of, and learnt that individual talent was all. We had the heavyweights – Crosby, Sinatra, Garland, Astaire, Kelly, etc. This made possible the more intimate and personal film. We then moved into the realm of the book musical – *Pal Joey, West Side Story, My Fair Lady, The Sound of Music, Half a Sixpence*, etc. In the future, I hope and believe, we will be able to make more mature stories with music.

Location work involving musical numbers must present considerable problems?

Making musicals on location is *hell*, but the only way you can capture the beauty and the authentic scene. You can't do it against a painted drop any longer. The advancement of colour photography and our abilities to create the 'magic' makes outdoor shooting the greatest of all challenges, and the most rewarding.

Do you find noticeable differences between working conditions in Britain and the United States?

Yes. *Half a Sixpence* was the first large-scale musical to be made in Britain. It was even necessary to import certain pieces of equipment and personnel. There was no classification for a music editor, and there had previously been no need for this specialized talent. The music editor we imported trained a group of British editors in this important work, and these are now carrying on teaching others, and have formed a new breed. We also imported a writer, director/producer, music supervisor, production designer/art director, and film editor. All these people had had extensive experience in the past working on the 'Hollywood musical'. They were integrated with British technicians and all became quite a happy family.

Could you describe some of the technicalities of shooting a big musical number in, say, Half a Sixpence?

All music and singing is pre-recorded. After the initial concept has been reached, a number goes through the following metamorphoses:

1. Concept
2. Rehearsal hall – dummy run with dance-ins
3. Composer – organize musical requirements
4. Conceive wardrobe – make-up
5. Musical sketch
6. Orchestrate
7. Rehearse all musical pieces
8. Record number
9. Edit all tracks – master dubbing and clicked playback track for shooting
10. Rehearse to pre-recorded track
11. Shoot
12. Edit
13. Musically sweeten and overdub
14. Musical sound effects and tapes
15. Final stereo dubbing

These are broadly the steps. There are many more facets than outlined, for example, the problems of where to rehearse – it is necessary to mock-up the set, props and wardrobe.

We shot the 'Banjo' number from *Half a Sixpence* in the theatre at Wimbledon, Surrey. It was necessary to rebuild the stage, enlarging and reinforcing it. We could shoot only in the daytime, as there was a show playing at night. We were forced to move our equipment out every night, replace the seats that had been removed to make room for our cameras, booms, etc. We had to establish places to feed the entire company. This is all a matter of logistics. It becomes like a military movement. Also, we had to bring huge portable generators to supply our lights. In addition, parking, transport and a thousand and one other details had to be planned and met.

The 'Flash, Bang, Wallop' number was shot in a studio. However, it was not possible to supply us with a proper stage and we were forced to work in a corrugated iron shed, with no facilities for air-conditioning. The heat became unbearable – dancers fainted. We tore off the side of the building to get air. When dancers are working, they get drenched, then they have to wait until the next set-up is ready. You can't just allow these people to get cold – muscles will become lame. So transitional areas had to be provided.

'If the Rain's Got to Fall' was filmed at Henley-on-Thames. We ran into foul weather. The Thames overflowed and we were bogged down in eight feet of mud. We were forced to build a road into the location, and then cover it with gravel and airport meshing. We erected a caravan and tent village to service the needs of the company. We hired two large Thames river excursion boats – one to be our dining-room, the other for the dancers to get out of their wet clothes and dry out. We lost all the real grass – it couldn't hold up under the dancing. We laid green cement and camouflage. We planted flowers, grass mats, trees, and fed the swans. We imported rain-making equipment so we could have rain where, when, and in the quantity we needed. It was necessary to establish a ferrying service to get large crowds, crew and equipment back and forth. The film took approximately a year and a half to make, including sixteen round-trips between Heathrow and Los Angeles.

The above are a few problems connected with one particular picture. The list in general could be extended indefinitely –

taking portable fog to San Francisco – carrying rain equipment through Britain – getting rid of telly aerials on 300-year-old thatched cottages – finding flowers in winter – coping with love scenes between husbands and wives – love scenes between lovers – love scenes between haters – making a pussy cat act – making a baby lovable – making people masculine, feminine, sexy, strong, weak, funny, tragic, cry, sing, dance, and most important of all, 'act natural' – it means answering a myriad problems to make everything moonlight and roses.

Fred Zinnemann

Fred Zinnemann (Austria) was born in 1907, and has worked in the United States since 1930, first as a film extra, then as a screenwriter and director of shorts. He has directed the following feature films: *Waves* (1935); *Kid Glove Killer* (1942); *Eyes in the Night* (1942); *The Seventh Cross* (1944); *Little Mr Jim* (1946); *My Brother Talks to Horses* (1947); *The Search* (1948); *Act of Violence* (1949); *The Men* (1950); *Teresa* (1951); *High Noon* (1952); *Member of the Wedding* (1952); *From Here to Eternity* (1953); *Oklahoma!* (1955); *A Hatful of Rain* (1957); *The Nun's Story* (1959); *The Sundowners* (1960); *Behold a Pale Horse* (1963); *A Man for All Seasons* (1966).

'The director, particularly of American films, has much, much more power and freedom today than he had during the anonymous days when films were made on the assembly line and slogans used to read, "If it's a Paramount picture, it's the best show in town." Quite often, as in my own case, he is able to choose, subject to budget limitations, his own subject, a large part of the cast, and most of the technicians. It is a curious fact, however, as *Cahiers du Cinéma* has pointed out, that in spite of all the constraints, some of the finest American films were made during that earlier period of around 1930–42.'

You keep very firm control on all aspects of the film you are working on?

Yes, starting with the script. To me, there are four basic, essential phases of the making of a film: (1) script; (2) planning (casting, production design, selection of locations, etc.); (3) filming; (4) editing. All these are inseparable, and all must be closely controlled by the director if the finished film is to be 'his' picture.

Do you keep closely to your script when shooting, or improvise to a certain extent?

I like to go on the floor with a script which is fairly detailed in terms of character development and character relationships, and thereafter I do a fair amount of improvisation.

In the same way, I like to give my cast a lot of freedom and room for experimentation in rehearsals. I try to get genuinely talented actors for every part in the film. It doesn't matter to me personally whether they are stars or not, or whether they have a great deal of experience or not, so long as their talent and instinct are strong. The more the actor contributes to the picture, the better, provided it is done within the confines of the characterization on which he and I have agreed beforehand. I don't believe in changing the treatment of a script to suit a particular star who might be available. I dislike holding a tight rein on anyone, and I look for the maximum contribution, not only from the actors, but equally from the production designer, cameraman, editor, and others. The more initiative and individual talent is brought into play from all sides, the better – provided it all harmonizes and balances in the end.

Do you rehearse much beforehand?

It depends. I like to rehearse some films fairly thoroughly, six to eight days in the main sets, with the key props and key furniture: but there have been other cases where rehearsal would have stifled a sense of improvisation and spontaneity essential to those particular projects.

As a general rule, obviously dependent on the type of film, do you use many takes?

Generally I prefer as few as possible: I find that if one makes many takes of the same scene, the energy, spontaneity and vitality of the actor's performance tends to decrease very sharply and to be replaced by a sort of polished mechanical glibness.

If you still had the choice, would you prefer to film in colour or black-and-white? Which do you find the most difficult?

I prefer black-and-white for most subjects which deal with

close personal experience. It leaves a great deal of room for the audience's imagination, whereas colour sometimes tends to externalize and distract. Therefore, colour and working in colour is infinitely more difficult than black-and-white.

Terence Young

Terence Young (Britain) was born in 1915. He began his career as a screenwriter, and has directed the following films: *One Night with You* (1949); *Corridor of Mirrors* (1949); *Woman Hater* (1949); *They Were Not Divided* (1951); *The Valley of the Eagles* (1952); *The Frightened Bride* (1953); *Red Beret* (1954); *That Lady* (1955); *Safari* (1956); *Storm Over the Nile* (1956); *Zarak* (1957); *Action of the Tiger* (1957); *Serious Charge* (1959); *Too Hot to Handle* (1959); *As Dark as the Night* (1959); *Black Tights* (1960); *Dr No* (1963); *From Russia With Love* (1964); *The Amorous Adventures of Moll Flanders* (1965); *Thunderball* (1965); *Triple Cross* (1966); *The Poppy is Also a Flower* (1966); *Wait Until Dark* (1967); *Mayerling* (1968); *The Christmas Tree* (1969).

'The actors are the important part of any film, and it is in his handling of them that a director's main interest should lie. I don't think the ideal director is one who gives a very good performance behind the camera – like Josef von Sternberg, who was much more dramatic than anything which was going on in front. Unfortunately the camera was pointing the wrong way.'

What are your methods of directing actors?

I first read through the script with the cast on the set: very often I find that certain lines will need altering to suit a particular artist. I never rehearse a film in its entirety. This is a theatrical tradition: the essence of cinema is that it captures something *at the precise moment it is occurring*. If it is over-rehearsed it loses its immediacy. Quite often I even shoot such rehearsals as I do have – and if they don't work, it doesn't matter. In the same way I keep the number of takes down as low as possible. An actress such as Audrey Hepburn, a wonderful artist, will give a great performance the first two or three takes, but after half-a-dozen she becomes tired, and what she was able to contribute at first has gone. In addition a player may tend in later takes to react *before* he hears (for the sixth or seventh time) the line which should cause the reaction. I will often have several takes without the clapperboard preceding them. That damned great BANG at the start of an important scene is a menace. You can see the actors react to it, and then try to get back into the right emotional mood and feeling.

I don't shoot from many angles, and I try to cut my films in the camera. In any case, too much cutting can ruin an emotional scene. A director can easily be too clever with his cutting. The climactic scene from *Wait Until Dark* – a scene which made even the critics at the press show scream – shows a supposedly dead man leap out of nowhere and grab at the blind Audrey Hepburn. I originally filmed this sequence all in close-ups, with five different camera positions. It didn't work. So I tried again – photographing the entire scene in long-shot, showing the whole set, Audrey Hepburn going up the stairs of her apartment, shaking the door, finding it locked, thinking of the window, coming downstairs again, starting across the room, then bang! he grabs her. It was essential for the audience to see the whole room all the time, in order to shout, 'God! Where did he come from?' There wasn't a single cut in the final version, all that use of close-ups was an attempt to be too clever. Incidentally, I wanted to make *Wait Until Dark* in black-and-white, but Jack Warner said: 'You're crazy!' Colour is obligatory now, under the rule of television.

Do you prefer location work or the more controllable conditions of the studio?

Location – always. Partly because television has accustomed audiences so much to reality, but also because locations seem to make so much difference to the artists. In *Mayerling*, James Mason portrayed the Emperor Franz-Josef in his actual apartments in the Hofburg, Vienna. After a day or two Mason caught many of the old Emperor's mannerisms, and a quite extraordinary atmosphere grew up. The Viennese technicians, steeped in their country's history, would bring Mason one of the throne chairs to sit on while he waited to be called, and as he walked to his dressing-room they actually used to stand and bow. Something of the majesty of the surroundings affected us all – all the extra expense and added difficulties of location work are made worth while when something like that happens.

Do you ever use second units?

I see no objection at all to using them as long as it is not an important sequence, or one very emotionally involved in the story. The overturning of the coach and some shots of sleighs in the snow in *Mayerling* were both filmed by a second unit.

In Black Tights *you directed an all-ballet film. Did this present any particular problems?*

The chief problem was to avoid being too clever. You can't make a good ballet film by having a whole battery of cameras set up all over the place. I scarcely used a master shot throughout the picture. After the first showing I discovered I had far too many close-ups: it's obviously essential that in filming ballet you should show the dancers' hands and feet almost throughout. So I recut it, making use of much more medium- and long-shot material. The procedure was to pre-record all the music on tape before shooting, and this remained as the actual sound track. The dancers then performed to the sound track. Every little piece of the ballet has to be taken separately, sometimes only fifteen seconds in which they pick up the music and the dance. The main difficulty was for the dancers to fit their movements to the playback. What looked perfectly satisfactory to the eye when shot often proved all wrong when it came to editing. The dancers could never believe this – until they saw for themselves!

How would you compare working conditions in Britain, America and France?

In the nineteen-thirties making a film in Britain was fun. The whole crew consisted of about thirty men. In my latest film, *Mayerling*, our crew numbered 120. The business of film-making has become intolerably ponderous. There's no need for this. In Sweden Ingmar Bergman has a crew of fifteen to twenty at the most – everybody helps everybody else. This is how it should be – not a rigidly departmentalized undertaking. In my opinion the happiest country for the film-maker nowadays is

France. Technically, Hollywood is still the most efficient, particularly as regards studio organization. Crews work well together and very fast – but the whole set-up is ruled by iron-curtain divisions between the various grades. In Britain the industry is crushed by trade unionism, and I say this although in the old days, when their hold was not strong enough, I was a trade union organizer. English technicians are in many ways the equal of American, but they work much more slowly – they are much less involved. In the States every technician will have read the script before shooting begins. In Britain scripts are handed out, but not many people bother to read them. And at 5.55 p.m., whatever may be happening on the set, all lights are pulled. A lot of American producers and directors are now complaining about British working conditions, and as soon as British films stop making money in the United States, they will pull out – and British film-makers will feel the draught. Nowadays it's in France that film-making is fun.

Richard Lester

Richard Lester (U.S.A.) was born in 1932 and started his career in television. He worked for many years in Britain and has directed *It's Trad, Dad* (1961); *The Mouse on the Moon* (1963); *A Hard Day's Night* (1964); *The Knack* (1965); *Help!* (1965); *A Funny Thing Happened on the Way to the Forum* (1966); *How I won the War* (1967); *Petulia* (1967); *The Bed-Sitting Room* (1969).

'My first directing experience was making the film extracts for television comedy series, and later, advertising films. These demand a form of shorthand filming which I found valuable training, in fact I still make advertising films from time to time. The position of a director of feature films should be that of a total dictator over his material, with three basic functions: (1) to take an idea or a theme and say to himself, "Can I use this as a means of making a piece of entertainment or putting forward some point?"; (2) having worked things out with the writer, to cast the people – artists and technicians – best suited to express this idea, and to combine them into a unified force for the realization of *his* vision; and (3) finally to get rid of his own and everyone else's mistakes. This is the editing process, where he throws out the rubbish. In every film there's good stuff and awful stuff: it's his problem to get rid of the awful stuff. I know that wonderful films can be made without this overall supervision by the director, but it is his responsibility: I don't want to take the blame for other people's mistakes, or the credit for their successes. This doesn't mean I like to go breathing down everyone's neck all the time. While making *How I Won the War* for instance, I never saw the rushes until the shooting was finished. I left this entirely to my editor. But I think that film work throughout is craftsmanship rather than artistry except as regards the director, because art is not created by a committee but by a personal vision. Otherwise it's as if Picasso gave seventy-seven people brushes and said, "Get on with that bit of the canvas until I come back at three o'clock and see how you're doing." If the film is an art, it is owing to the director's vision.'

Do you allow your actors much freedom, within these limits, to develop their own characterizations, to improvise?

I hope I do. I never direct an actor by *showing* him what to do, not being an actor myself, but I try to lead him into creating my own idea of a character without being too specific. The Beatles were very carefully manipulated in their two films because they had had no acting experience. None of them had more than one line at a time. I do very little rehearsal – never before we get to the spot and never before the actual take. I merely see that the actors know what they say and where they are. This is because something exciting and unexpected may happen at any time and I don't want to lose it. I'm always prepared for the happy accident. It's for this reason I always leave blank spaces in my otherwise fairly complete scripts – room for improvisation. For instance, the moving bed sequence in *The Knack* was described in a couple of lines only: 'The bed goes through a car wash' or 'down the river'. Everything else was ad lib. I believe in a policy of catch-as-catch-can. This is one reason why I never work in a studio if I can help it. I prefer the surprises of location. Suddenly, when you arrive, it starts to rain – and you take advantage of that although in the script it's a fine day. When we were making the Beatles' films *A Hard Day's Night* and *Help!*, we would arrive on a street location and only have time to shoot one quick take before the news got around and huge crowds gathered so that we had to run off somewhere else and try again. On one occasion an entire school rushed from their classrooms and surrounded us. It was like going back to the old Hollywood silent days of grab a scene and run.

Do you select your own camera angles and set-ups?

Yes, all of them, and choose the lenses as well. I always use two cameras, sometimes more, and often operate one of them myself. I agree with Fritz Lang that a director must know the technicalities of everybody's job on a film – but he must then try not to exercise that knowledge: just as a conductor has to know how to play a violin even though he won't be as good a violinist as the poorest one in his orchestra.

Your first dramatic film, Petulia, *has been described on occasion as difficult to follow. Does a possible lack of complete communication worry you at all?*

The cinema has as much right to demand total attention from its audiences as any other art form. A director should not shrink from being 'difficult' if he feels it is necessary. I consider that the cinema is now obsolete because of television, and therefore has the responsibility of being an art form. The theatre only became an art form when it was itself made obsolete by the cinema.

Roman Polanski

Roman Polanski (Poland), was born in 1933 and began his career as an actor. He made several short fiction films before directing *Knife in the Water* (1962); *Repulsion* (1965); *Cul-de-Sac* (1966); *Dance of the Vampires* (*The Fearless Vampire Killers*) (1967); *Rosemary's Baby* (1969).

'After starting as an actor in Poland I made films in France, Poland, England, and recently in America. In Poland, film-making is a nationalized industry, with no individual drive for personal achievement. Consequently, as always in such cases, everything goes down – French television is a terrible example. Since 1955 there has been a tendency in Poland to free the arts medium, so that there is some competition on the artistic if not the material level – but the film-maker may still be unable to say what he wants to say. I came from France to England to make *Repulsion*, though in actual fact *Cul-de-Sac,* which was made later, was written first. I think the period of the early sixties in England was a great one for film production, a renaissance: but it didn't last long. Trade unionism is the factor which is killing the British film industry. To take just one example. In *Dance of the Vampires* there is a big ballroom scene, one of the climaxes of the film. We had special effects to prepare, and sixty difficult make-ups. The result was that we couldn't start shooting before noon, and were unable to complete the scene within the scheduled time. We had only five days left before the very elaborate set was due to be dismantled – broken up for good. So the producer started negotiating with the studio for overtime. It was very difficult, like having a knife held at one's throat, but eventually an agreement was arrived at for two or three hours' overtime during the following three to four days. Suddenly two chargehands revived an old argument with the studio about an extra sixpence an hour. These two men decided to strike. We pleaded with them, and they said, "We have nothing against you, but we must settle this argument." This meant that nobody else could work, and we could not shoot overtime – but we had to *pay* everybody overtime just the same, because they had already agreed to stay on. This is the sort of thing which is discouraging America from pouring any more money into British production. Nowadays if someone works fast, someone else says to him: "Don't run, be British!" That's the way to destroy an industry.

'In addition to this, there's no other country which has only two main cinema circuits – Rank and ABC. The result of this monopoly is that there are many valuable films which no one ever sees. The average filmgoer in a small town is kept in ignorance of what is being produced, and his taste is given no chance of widening and evolving.'

Do you work from a very full script?

As far as the action is concerned, yes; but I work out things like camera angles on the set. I rehearse the actors in the scene and then find the best angle from which to photograph them. I know some directors work the reverse way, but I could not do this myself. I improvise very little. To me it's a *faiblesse,* indicating either a lack of knowledge of your job, or just laziness. The characters are the most important thing in the cinema, and when I cast I look for the most suitable actors. If anyone finds a line or a situation difficult I will try to alter it, but I don't agree with saying: 'Okay guys, just sit down and do it.' That simply slows down the action.

What about takes, and cameras?

I use a lot of takes, many more than I shall need. Lots of waste. If a scene doesn't come out right after many takes you know something is wrong, and try alternatives. In *Dance of the Vampires* I sometimes made fifty to sixty takes of a scene – it can be very frustrating! I never use more than one camera, not even for an elaborate sequence, unless it is a question of safety which might make it risky to repeat an action. There's only one perfect angle from which to photograph – so only one camera. Nor would I ever make use of a second unit.

In three of your films which are concentrated very much in a single setting, Cul-de-Sac, Repulsion *and* Rosemary's Baby, *the viewer is made familiar to quite an unusual extent with that setting – particularly in the last two – as if he lived there himself, almost.*

I think it is very important in films such as *Repulsion* and *Rosemary's Baby* that this should be so. The audience should know without effort, when they are in one room or passage, exactly where the rest of the place is in relation to it, as if it was their own home. I spent a great deal of time in the early part of *Repulsion* in setting out the geography of the sisters' flat: in *Rosemary's Baby* we had the help of the janitor being able to take the young couple right through the apartment as an essential part of the plot.

Do you prefer colour or black-and-white?

Definitely colour. It's much harder work, but much more

satisfying. You can use it to enhance the atmosphere of a scene or to heighten dramatic effect by contrast, as I tried to do in *Rosemary's Baby*.

John Schlesinger

John Schlesinger (Britain) was born in 1926. He has worked as an actor, television director, and director of shorts (of which one, *Terminus*, won the Golden Lion award at Venice in 1961). His feature films are: *A Kind of Loving* (1962); *Billy Liar* (1963); *Darling* (1965); *Far From the Madding Crowd* (1967); *Midnight Cowboy* (1969); *Bloody Sunday* (1970).

'Making a film is like going down a mine: once you've started you bid a metaphorical good-bye to the daylight and the outside world for the duration. Or you might describe it as a tempestuous love affair. I don't see how a director can make a satisfactory film unless he is most deeply emotionally involved. I sometimes wish I could make a film with less agonizing and more exuberance, but if I did I imagine I should finish up even less content with the result than I am now.'

Did you find your early work on television a help when you came to make feature films?

It certainly taught me to develop my powers of observation and to make decisions quickly. The speed at which you are obliged to work teaches you a sort of basic film grammar; like weekly repertory in the theatre does for an actor. The time factor is so limited that one's first impressions of something are usually the last, and this was useful. My work on documentaries was also helpful, particularly *Terminus*, a film about Waterloo Station, on which I was given a great deal of freedom. My experience as an actor was valuable also because, having been on the other side of the fence, I know how an actor feels and how much help or encouragement he or she may need at a particular moment. It's essential that a director should be something of a psychologist – not only with actors but with everyone who is working with him. It's his function to control all the different elements by collaboration, not dictatorship. That's one reason I like using the same cameraman, art director, actors, composer, when possible.

By 'control' you mean a fairly firm hand on every aspect of the production?

The director's job is to be the artist behind the whole conception, so he must have the first and final choice of everything. I watch over all stages of a film, including post-synching, which I think needs as careful direction as the original shooting. We considerably improved one particular performance in *Far From the Madding Crowd* at this stage.

Do you improvise?

To a certain extent. I don't believe that one should ever be slavish to the script if it doesn't sound right at rehearsal, unless one is working with a particularly stylized piece of dialogue. In *Midnight Cowboy* (1969) we used improvisation a great deal during the pre-shooting rehearsals. The author of the screenplay, Waldo Salt, and I would come to rehearsal with a tape-recorder, and after we had run through the scenes as they were written, with Dustin Hoffman and the rest of the cast, we would suggest further ideas about the characters they were playing, and encourage them to improvise on those lines. Interesting points often emerged, which we were able to include in the final screenplay. This was the first time I used this particular technique.

Three of your films, Billy Liar, A Kind of Loving *and* Far From the Madding Crowd, *were adaptations from well-known works: did you refer much to the originals?*

I think it's better for someone other than the author to do an adaptation. You get a fresh viewpoint. In the case of *Far From the Madding Crowd*, of course, this question did not arise. Hardy would have been a splendid writer for the screen. His books are so filled with visual imagery and symbolism that there were many places in *Far From the Madding Crowd* where the text would suggest the way to approach a sequence visually. What we tried to do was to convey the inner feeling of Hardy's philosophy – the power of nature, the wrath of providence – his sense of proportion, so beautifully conveyed, for instance, in the scene where Bathsheba, suffering under her great trouble, watches the petty problems of a little boy trying to learn his Sunday collect.

Do you prefer working in colour to working in black-and-white?

Far From the Madding Crowd was my first colour film. I wish it wasn't so compulsory, owing to the demands of television. Some subjects demand colour and some black-and-white. There should be a choice.

Do you find the new freedom of technique stimulating?

I much admire directors such as Dick Lester and Jean-Luc Godard who have extended the freedom of the cinema. But I sometimes think technique has run away with itself. Very often people are more interested in technique than in actual content. I am not. I like to make films about people, and leave room for performance. I don't leave a film of Antonioni's admiring particularly the performances, and I don't believe that an actress like Monica Vitti is allowed to act in his films so much as to display a personality used in a certain way by the director. Too much concern for technique is apt to turn actors into puppets. I'm more interested in characters, in human beings, than in new methods of photographing them. And of course there's very little that is really new. The split screen was used by D. W. Griffith, the triple screen by Abel Gance.

You have considerable control over your film while you are making it – but afterwards?

The position is very unsatisfactory. Take colour, for example. After we have gone to enormous trouble to match the various shots, everything can be changed in the laboratories, and there is nothing the director or the cameraman can do about it – not even about the changes of values between reels which may ruin the whole effect of their work. Visconti made a fuss about the bad colour matching in *The Leopard,* but without any success. Also cuts: every film I have made seems to have been cut by the distributors, particularly in the United States. A scene in *Billy Liar* was removed without consultation by the American distributor, simply because he felt that it made Billy look unsympathetic. Despite contractual obligations, MGM decided to make cuts in *Far From the Madding Crowd* at first without consultation with us, though it was the producer and myself who felt the need to shorten it. One has little redress, except to become more difficult and demanding. My own emotional involvement in a film lasts until it is exposed to its first audience. Then it evaporates. But this does not mean a director loses all interest in how his film is treated afterwards. William Wyler, for instance, once went to see an old film of his at a drive-in cinema, was dissatisfied with one scene, and wanted to recall all the prints in order to re-cut it!

The worst part of film-making? The moment of decision when you don't know how to solve a particular problem on the set, and the technicians are standing around waiting for you to make up your mind. You have to resist the terrible pressure at such moments to hurry – and take the wrong step.

Otto Preminger

Otto Preminger (Austria) was born in 1906. He directed a number of films before moving to Hollywood, and has also worked as a theatrical director. His feature films are: *Under Your Spell* (1936); *Danger* (1937); *Love at Work* (1937); *Margin for Error* (1943); *In the Meantime, Darling* (1944); *Laura* (1944); *A Royal Scandal* (1945); *Fallen Angel* (1945); *Centennial Summer* (1946); *Forever Amber* (1947); *Daisy Kenyon* (1947); *The Fan* (1949); *Whirlpool* (1949); *Where the Sidewalk Ends* (1950); *The Thirteenth Letter* (1950); *Angel Face* (1953); *The Moon is Blue* (1953); *River of No Return* (1954); *Carmen Jones* (1954); *The Court Martial of Billy Mitchell* (1955); *The Man with the Golden Arm* (1955); *Saint Joan* (1957); *Bonjour Tristesse* (1958); *Porgy and Bess* (1959); *Anatomy of a Murder* (1959); *Exodus* (1960); *Advise and Consent* (1962); *The Cardinal* (1963); *In Harm's Way* (1965); *Bunny Lake is Missing* (1965); *Hurry Sundown* (1966); *Skidoo!* (1969); *Tell Me That You Love Me, Junie Moon* (1970).

'I believe that any change in a creative profession is eventually beneficial, because changing means growing and living. Even a change for the worse gives the critical mind food for thought and might cause further changes for the better.'

Did you find your theatrical background a help when you began to direct films?

Naturally, I found anything in my background helpful, be it

directing in the theatre or acting on the stage and in films, but it is important for the director to keep the basic technical differences between the two media always in mind.

Do you keep a very close hand on all the processes of your films?

The direction of the editor, the script-writer, the cameraman, the art director, and all other craftsmen who contribute to the film, is just as vitally important as the direction of the actors, although the latter is generally considered the director's main task.

Do you like to rehearse before going on the floor?

Yes.

Do you improvise much, or keep closely to the script?

I generally follow the script.

Many of your films have been adaptations of well-known novels or plays. Do you confer much with the author, if he is available, or approach the work from an entirely new angle?

Whenever possible, I discuss the script with the original author. However, I consider film the director's medium, and with the acquisition of rights I don't feel obligated to be 'faithful' to the original. The original story, theme and characters become the director's raw material. They are being filtered through his brain, emotions and whatever talents he has, and he is entitled to the credit for the success of the film and must bear the whole blame for its failure.

It has been said of you that 'in leaving us to notice actions and wonder about the motivation behind them, Preminger is demanding the same level of audience participation as Antonioni. There is a similar refusal to explain emotions to the audience. Both show us evidence and make us draw the conclusions.'[2] Would you consider this a correct comment?

I am leaving this judgement to my critics.

But you think, as a director, that it is more satisfactory for an audience to have to do some of its own thinking rather than have everything pointed out to them?

To stimulate the thinking of an audience means entertaining them just as much as making them laugh or cry.

2. *Movie 2.*

What would you consider the greatest asset for a young director today to possess? What are the prospects for him?

To answer this question, somebody – not I – would have to write a book.

J. Lee-Thompson

J. Lee-Thompson (Britain) was born in 1914 and started in films as a screenwriter. The feature films which he has directed are: *Murder Without Crime* (1950); *The Yellow Balloon* (1952); *The Weak and the Wicked* (1954); *For Better, For Worse* (1954); *As Long as They're Happy* (1955); *An Alligator Named Daisy* (1955); *Yield to the Night* (1956); *The Good Companions* (1957); *Woman in a Dressing-Gown* (1957); *Ice Cold in Alex* (1958); *No Trees in the Street* (1959); *Tiger Bay* (1959); *Northwest Frontier* (1959); *The Guns of Navarone* (1961); *Cape Fear* (1962); *Taras Bulba* (1962); *Kings of the Sun* (1963); *What a Way to Go!* (1964); *John Goldfarb Please Come Home* (1965); *Return from the Ashes* (1965); *Eye of the Devil* (1966); *Before Winter Comes* (1968); *MacKenna's Gold* (1968); *The Most Dangerous Man in the World* (1969); *Country Dance* (1969).

'The knack of choosing his scripts wisely is one of the greatest assets a director can have – knowing what to discard, what to refuse. I've learnt by experience that it's fatal to accept a poor script because it contains one or two good scenes which you long to shoot! My advice to any young director who has had his first big success would be – resist the flood of scripts which will probably start pouring in on you: sit back and wait for the next *good* subject to come along. I think there are many potentially successful directors who have started well, chosen badly and then fallen by the wayside. After making a number of films with themes of sociological significance, such as the anti-capital-punishment *Yield to the Night*, still one of my own favourites, I branched out into the commercial field and made a number of pictures of which I am not at all proud. That can happen to a director!'

You have a particular liking for films of suspense?

Good suspense stories are not easy to find, but when they do

come along they can be very satisfying. Suspense is a major in-
gredient of the film. Tension can be tightened and sustained to a
greater extent in the cinema than in either the theatre or the
novel. It is partly what cinema is all about. In the early days it
stood for 'romance' – now for suspense, in all its varying
forms.

*Do you find that your considerable experience as a script-
writer has been an advantage as a director?*

Very much so, largely in the development of character. You
have to condense so much for films that a great deal has to
register in a very short time. This has to be achieved without the
result seeming 'plotty', and there just isn't the opportunity
which you have in the theatre for exploring depths of character.
Having written myself, I realize some of the snags which can
arise in developing a screen story, and this has helped me enormously when, as director, I came to shooting one.

*Do you use this experience to work closely on scripts you are
directing, but have not written yourself?*

Only when this has been agreed from the start, or where I am
working in collaboration. I never try to rewrite another
author's words, I merely go to him and suggest what I feel
might be changed with advantage.

Do you work from a very detailed script, and adhere to it?

I don't like to be given technical suggestions such as camera
set-ups. I'll work these out for myself. I take a scene, prepare it,
and literally map it out camera angle by camera angle as I see it
in my mind's eye. But I'll always alter it if the actors feel uncomfortable. I allow them as much freedom as is consistent
with preserving the mood of a scene. I think it's vitally important that a director should always consider his actors – in fact I
would go so far as to say that a good director must *love* actors
(in spite of the fact that Hitchcock, one of the very greatest of
all, is famous for his hatred of them, for regarding them as an
evil necessity!).

Many of the biggest stars I have worked with are full of
doubts and insecurity. The director must be sensitive to their
problems, and able to build up their self-confidence. He may be
just as nervous and insecure himself, but it's his job to fight

through this and, in fact, to be something of a nursemaid to the cast who have thrown in their lot with him.

Have you much freedom in your choice of cast?

Within limits. If a studio is going to spend $5,000,000 on a picture they will, understandably, insist on having a say in the choice of stars. Not infrequently a director may have a fine script which he knows is right for a comparatively unrecognized actor, but he will find difficulty in obtaining financial backing for it. He will end up casting it with an actor who is not so right for it, because he has a big name and big names bring in the cash. The parrot-cry that the star system is dead is all nonsense, you only have to try to raise money for a production to discover that. Thousands of exhibitors all over the world still look down the list of films available, note the star names and say 'He (or she) is popular at my cinema' – booking the picture without seeing it, on this count alone.

You have fairly definite views on producers?

If you mean the producer who is always breathing down a director's neck, I have. Worst of all is the type who undermines his director's confidence, often causing him to pass on this sense of insecurity to his cast. Too often in this business the producer is a hindrance to a director – he doesn't know how to shoot a foot of film, and is in fact a megalomaniac able only to interfere with the director's work and undermine his influence. This applies not only to the actual shooting period, but afterwards in the cutting-room. You have shot a film in a certain way because you know what you want. How can a producer, coming in afterwards as some of them do and editing *your* film – how can he possibly read what was in your mind? It's not your film any longer unless you have kept a very firm hand on this all-important process – aided of course by your own editor, who follows your own ideas, and often helps them by fresh suggestions.

On the other hand, the producer who is loyal to his director – who may have any number of stormy meetings with him over finance and other matters in private, but backs him up, whatever the circumstances, on the set – is an inestimable help. I am only thankful there are so many of them.

What do you think the future holds for the cinema industry, and the film as an art?

The cinema is growing up very gradually, and I think this slow pace is a good thing. Many people look on the film as a great art form. It isn't. It's a great mass medium for entertainment. Too often this is forgotten, especially by many brilliant younger directors. The habit of 'going to the cinema' has gone. Give the public what they want and they'll come in greater numbers than ever before – but what is the use of the most high-minded film if – because the makers have forgotten that they are working in a mass entertainment medium – it plays to empty seats?

Jack Cardiff

Jack Cardiff (Britain) was born in 1914 and started his career as a child actor. He became a cameraman, and eventually director of photography for many well-known feature films, including *Black Narcissus* (1946, directed by Michael Powell and Emeric Pressburger) which won an Academy Award. Since becoming a director he has made the following films: *Intent to Kill* (1957); *Beyond this Place* (1958); *Scent of Mystery* (1959); *Sons and Lovers* (1960); *My Geisha* (1961); *The Lion* (1962); *The Long Ships* (1963); *Young Cassidy* (1964); *The Liquidator* (1965); *The Mercenaries* (1967); *Girl on a Motorcycle* (1968).

'After a good many years as a cameraman myself I found at first that working as a director, in close contact with another cameraman, was a little embarrassing. I was always particularly careful never to suggest how a scene should be lit, using a mixture of tact and cunning to make the cameraman think he was doing it all on his own! From this it might seem the ideal arrangement to take on both jobs together, but this is totally exhausting. A director is always in conflict with somebody, actors or technicians – generally actors – and to have to combine his conflicts with the cameraman's conflicts is too much for one human being to cope with!'

Have you returned to camera work since you started directing?

Once. I was lighting cameraman on *Fanny* after directing *Sons and Lovers*, and I think it worked out all right. But despite my great admiration for Joshua Logan I found it very frustrating, and I would never do it again.

Do you use a multi-camera technique, and many takes?

I use as few cameras as possible unless for something unrepeatable, like the real train wreck in *The Mercenaries*, where I used as many as I could get, which, on location, was four.

As I think is the case with most directors nowadays, I like if possible to 'cut with the camera'. A lot of producers prefer the old-fashioned technique of starting a scene with a 'cover shot', a long shot, which records the whole scene, followed by close-ups, then over-the-shoulder shots, in other words, covering from every possible angle, after which the cutter will go to work on this mass of material, with an infinite number of permutations. This is the safe way of doing it, enabling you to cut out any unwanted lines, overlay dialogue, speed up or slow down the tempo, and always have the master shot to refer back to. I think the producer's preference for this method is due to the fact that many of them are frustrated directors, and it at least allows them plenty of leeway to edit the picture as they think fit, once the director has had his 'first cut' and been dismissed!

Clearly on a very important picture you must play for safety and cover yourself with a few close-ups, but when I can I like to work the opposite way – make myself familiar with the mood and tempo of a scene, then visualize it already cut as I'm shooting. In fact, I have often done only one take and got away with it – and often, I must confess, done only one take and *not* got away with it, regretting afterwards that I hadn't any covering shots to bridge an awkward moment. As far as the actors are concerned, it's a matter of compromise. Some are perfect for about three takes then begin to get tired, to forget their lines: others get better after about fifteen – you have to strike a balance. Sometimes I will shoot a rehearsal, to the annoyance of the technicians who complain they have had no time to rehearse their own jobs!

When working on a film from a well-known book, such as Sons and Lovers, *do you refer much to the book?*

I made *Sons and Lovers* with the screenplay under one arm and the book under the other. Quite often an actor would say he felt uncomfortable about speaking some line in the script – it didn't feel right. I would refer to the book and there, in its original form, was the perfect line. Many scriptwriters, receiving their high salaries, feel constrained to change a book just for the sake of doing so – turning it inside out and back to front, leaving not a single line of the original dialogue. This is frequently quite unnecessary. There are novels which are almost screenplays in themselves, but let a scriptwriter be handed one and there won't be much of it left.

Do you adhere closely to your script, or improvise?

I always work from a very full dialogue script. If possible I have a round-table conference with the writer, and will not bring up again the points settled then. I don't believe in improvisation, unless it is essential, because of the expense. With money, whether pounds or dollars, ticking away at the rate it does in a film studio, you shouldn't be using up time discussing with an actor some phrase which he would like to word differently. If there are to be such discussions they should take place in the dressing-room during waits while the lights are set up, or away from the set altogether. Ideally, leading members of the cast should be in on round-table conferences, where they can raise their objections or make their often very valuable suggestions, which can then be dealt with, and the final form fixed. This is frequently impossible because at that time they will be working elsewhere. On location, of course, things are easier, particularly if, as in the case of *Girl on a Motorcycle*, you have a very small crew. In these circumstances, half an hour's off-the-cuff discussion and alteration does not mean the waste of a large amount of the producer's money, and you can to a certain extent indulge in the luxury of improvisation.

Do you allow your actors much freedom, or hold them with a fairly firm rein?

This is the hardest question of all to answer. Obviously it must depend to a large extent on the actor concerned. There is always *some* conflict between a director and his cast, who naturally have their own preconceived ideas. While working as

cameraman with a number of directors of the highest standing,
I learnt from them a number of invaluable lessons in handling
actors, and one of the most important was the art of hypocrisy.
Very few actors can take criticism unless it is well concealed in
a sugar coating. 'That was marvellous, absolutely marvellous!
There's just one tiny point I think we might consider altering
slightly . . .'

Whenever possible, I compromise, so long as this is worked
out before we go on the set. Once there, the director's word
must be law – which most actors recognize. One of my
strongest rules is that I am the only person to say 'Cut!' The all-
important word belongs to one man – the director.

Peter Hall

Peter Hall (Britain) was born in 1930. In 1954 he was appointed
director of the Arts Theatre, London, and in 1960, director of the
Royal Shakespeare Company. He has directed the following feature
films: *Work Is a Four Letter Word* (1967); *A Midsummer Night's
Dream* (1968); *Three Into Two Won't Go* (1969); *Perfect Friday*
(1970).

'The dangerous difference between directing in the theatre and
directing in films lies in the change of work rhythm. You have
to learn to condense the theatre's six-week rehearsal period on a
speech into half an hour. In film directing you prepare a scene,
rehearse, bring the actors to the boil and keep them there, all in
a very short time. Then it's fixed for ever. It's really a completely different process. You haven't time for trial and error in
making a film. In the theatre you can give an arbitrary direction
to an actor and he will go home and digest it, and perhaps use it
the following day when he has made it his own. No creative
actor works well by external direction. The final interpretation
has got to be his own. In the cinema, with perhaps twenty
minutes at your disposal, an arbitrary direction will remain
external, outside the player, so it is necessary to work by suggestion, stimulation and improvisation, rather than the slow exam-
ination of one possibility after another.

'It's important for me to rehearse for a short time before going near a camera, partly because of the lack of continuity, partly because you don't have enough time to give to the actors "on the floor". We rehearsed *Work Is a Four Letter Word* for a fortnight straight through for intentions only, not moves: *A Midsummer Night's Dream* for a week in the loosest kind of way, discussing each scene as we went along on the location.

'Another difficulty facing the film director who comes from the theatre is that of keeping himself afloat during the waits. In the theatre I am working at absolutely full capacity from the moment I go on the stage until the moment I leave it. In the film studio there are long periods when I can do nothing while the technicians take over – forty-five minutes, an hour, even two hours during which the director has to go away, read a paper, phone his wife, eat a sausage – and then come back and carry on where he left off.

'Great acting is great acting whatever the medium, and the cinema betrays clichés or cheating in performance in a far more deadly manner than the theatre. The screen reveals dishonesty instantly. The two are not really comparable as art forms. Both their public and the means of communication by which they reach that public are totally different. Both are equally valid, but the medium of our time is the cinema.'

As a director of long standing in the theatre, do you prefer working in the studio, as having more in common with the stage, to location?

I hate studios *because* they are like the theatre. Films have nothing to do with 'the stage'. On location the camera selects from reality. However good a studio set may be, its mere existence is already an act of selectivity, so that the camera is merely recording something already selected. You lose the texture, and the surprise. No art director can give you a wall as real as a real wall. If he did, you'd say he had overdone it. Even with interiors, I prefer locations, with all their added difficulties.

What are your views on putting Shakespeare on the screen?

I don't agree with large-scale Shakespearean films, where the lines are cut for the sake of the spectacle. The only reason for

1. Part of the art department at Pinewood Studios. Art director Ken Adams is putting the finishing touches to some of his sketches for *Chitty Chitty Bang Bang*.
2. Director of photography Douglas Slocombe on the set for *The Lion in Winter*.

3. Pinewood Studios, the monopole overhead lighting system on the new L stage, opened in May 1969.

4. Pinewood Studios, L and M stages. The stages are dual purpose, for television and feature film productions. The whole of the lighting system is controlled from above the stage, and specially designed lightweight lamps, which give a greater light source than traditional studio lamps, have been installed. The lights are controlled from a console which includes dimmer controls and the possible use of a lighting memory system.

5. Pinewood Studios, the vacuum press shop. The vacuum press moulds sheets of PVC for film sets, making reproductions of bricks, stone, roof slates, tiles, timber and boarding six times as fast as traditional methods. The illustrations show: (top left) machine with safety screen down; (top right) placing plastic sheeting over stone mould; (bottom left) sheeting being cut after impression; (bottom right) finished pressing being examined and ready for final trim—some examples of other pressings can be seen in the top right of this photograph.

6. (Above left) Pinewood Studios, one of the vast 165′ × 110′ stages. A fantasy space-ship is being constructed for *Tomorrow*, at present in the course of production.

7. London crescent set for *Oliver*, designed by John Box. The site, at Shepperton Studios, was chosen because of the oak trees, as they would anchor the set; a location could not be used as present-day styles would have conflicted with the Dickensian period, and because it would not have been possible to stop the daily life on a real location for the five to six week period needed for rehearsal on the set. (Above) the set completed on the eve of shooting; (below) the set under construction.

8. London street set for *Oliver*, designed by John Box. (Above left) the set being marked out before construction; (above right) the set under construction; (below) the set during the course of shooting.

9. The house at Varykino, built for *Dr Zhivago*, and designed by John Box. The house was built during the autumn so that when the actual winter conditions came it would still be possible to maintain the effect the director wanted. The house was also required for spring and summer sequences: the plaster snow cladding was then removed to reveal the normal roof and walls underneath (see chapter 6).

10. On location for *Lawrence of Arabia*. Ali (Omar Sharif) appears out of the mirage (see chapter 6).

11. Building a space-ship for *2001: A Space Odyssey* (production designers: Tony Masters, Harry Lange, Ernie Archer).
12. On location for *The Last Grenade* in Hong Kong. Director Gordon Flemyng (seated centre) watches Honor Blackman during a take, while Stanley Baker says his lines off camera.
13. Director Richard Attenborough on location for *Oh! What a Lovely War*.

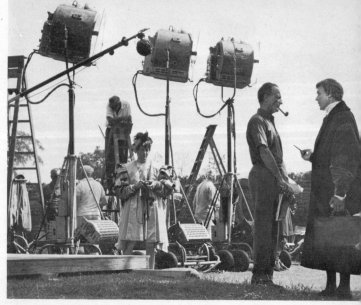

14. John Frankenheimer directing *The Fixer*.
15. Director and actor: Fred Zinnemann and Paul Scofield on the set for *A Man for All Seasons*.
16. Director and actor: Lindsay Anderson discusses a close-up for *If . . .* with Malcolm McDowell.

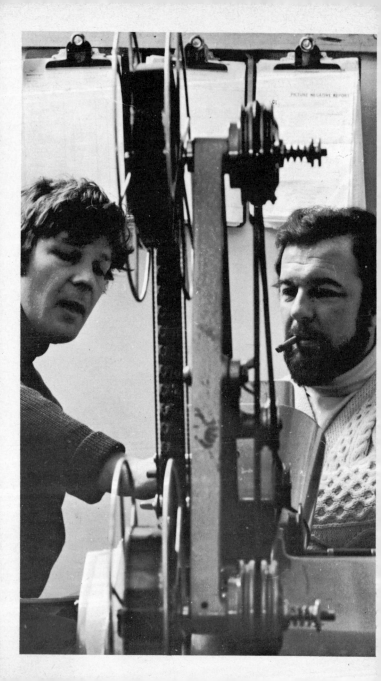

17. Director and editor: Peter Hall and Rex Pyke working on *Perfect Friday* in the cutting-room (photo Ron Reid).
18. The exterior tank at Pinewood Studios in use during the filming of *When Eight Bells Toll*. The actual exterior of the caves was shot on location in Scotland.

19. The train derailment in *Lawrence of Arabia*. (Below) Cliff Richardson paces the distance to check that the timing of the explosion will be correct, while one of his assistants places the charges; (right) the actual explosion.

20. The multi-barrel capsule gun designed by Cliff Richardson for simulating bullet ricochets.
21. In *Jason and the Argonauts*, Ray Harryhausen's 'dynamation' process combines fantastic models with real people.
22. Ray Harryhausen with his model of a prehistoric animal.

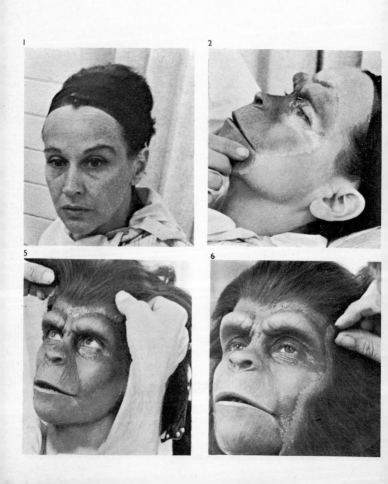

23. The transformation of Kim Hunter for *Planet of the Apes* (photos by courtesy of Twentieth Century-Fox).

24. A still from *Trans-Europ-Express*, at present refused a certificate by the censor (photo by courtesy of the distributors, Connoisseur Films).

filming Shakespeare is that the camera can bring him closer to the audience, and enable them to hear and understand the ambiguity and flexibility of his text more easily than in the theatre. I shot *A Midsummer Night's Dream* largely in huge close-up and with almost a full text, cutting on the end of the line or on the caesura. I tried to match the picture rhythm to the verse rhythm, but breaking the rule now and again as Shakespeare did to show both his humanity and his freedom from rigid formality. In the final analysis I don't believe Shakespeare can work in film – the finest Shakespearean films have been best as films when they were being least Shakespearean – that is visual, not verbal.

Coming fairly recently from the theatre to film-making, how do you feel about present conditions and future prospects?

The high profits of the cinema attract a lot of producers who would do extremely well in the Mafia, but have no creative instincts whatever. The whole process at present is both over-expensive and over-financed. On the technical side, I am amazed at the cumbersome nature of film-making, the sheer size of the equipment and of the unit. It will be an enormous advantage if one day we can work always in 16 mm., with a sufficiently improved stock to blow up to 35 mm. without loss of quality. And I think one of the most vital improvements would be that a director could see an instant playback of what he had shot. The technique is developed, but it is not used.

I think that the cinema as we know it is on the way out: in ten years' time people will have a collection of long-play visuals on tape of their favourite films, which they will play back on their television sets. This method of home film viewing will provide increased opportunities for the small budget picture – that will be its saving grace.

Tony Richardson

Tony Richardson (Britain) was born in 1928. He is a television and stage director, and has directed the following feature films: *Look Back in Anger* (1959); *The Entertainer* (1959); *Sanctuary* (1960); *A Taste of Honey* (1961); *The Loneliness of the Long Distance Runner*

98   The Making of Feature Films

(1962); *Tom Jones* (1963); *The Loved One* (1965); *Mademoiselle* (1966); *The Sailor from Gibraltar* (1967); *Red and Blue* (1968); *The Charge of the Light Brigade* (1968); *Laughter in the Dark* (1969); *Hamlet* (1969); *Ned Kelly* (1970).

'I think it is no help at all for a film director to have had previous experience in the theatre – rather the opposite. Very few people have made the change successfully. The theatre is a literary tradition, and I have always had to fight to overcome a literary approach to film-making because of my work in it. The two roles are entirely different. In the theatre the director is in a solely interpretative position – interpreting what the playwright has written. However brilliantly he may do this, he creates nothing himself. In the cinema the director is the creative artist – ultimately responsible for what goes on the screen. A script which is of little worth in itself can be created into a great film by the director. There is no doubt, as far as I am concerned, that the cinema is the more satisfying medium. Making a film is, for the director, an entirely original act, from the moment of kicking a subject around, through the processes of shooting, editing, sound mixing – to the final master print.'

Do you work from a very detailed script, and adhere to it?

I generally start off with a detailed *dialogue* script, but I tend to change a lot of it on the floor. Hitchcock, who works everything out beforehand in the most minute detail, once said to me: 'The fun of making a film is in the imagination of what I'm going to do. The shooting is just an anticlimax.' Antonioni works out every shot with stand-ins first. For me it's the other way round: the shooting is the really creative part, when you're actually handling the paint, so to speak, not putting down something conceptual, but the actual conception itself.

For this reason also I tend to avoid holding many rehearsals. Very often the best moments in a performance are spontaneous – some small sudden movement or unexpected reaction – and in filming you are able to catch that immediate moment and preserve it. Partly, of course, this depends on the actors. An actor may be temperamentally unable to adapt to quick changes – give him an unexpected cue and it throws him. On the other hand you can hand a whole new scene to, say, John Gielgud, and he will adapt himself to it at a moment's notice. It's a question of different methods. Jean-Luc Godard, as Anna Karina told me, rehearses, rehearses, rehearses. Laurence Olivier also spends a lot of time on rehearsal. I myself will do so on occasion: for *Look Back in Anger*, a very literary script, we rehearsed a full week. In the case of *Laughter in the Dark* I also rehearsed very fully, because two of the cast were French and were playing in English, and the importance of their feeling secure in their lines was obviously paramount. Given the choice, however, I prefer spontaneity.

Similarly, I always work on location in preference to the studio. On location, at any time, a miracle may happen – some entirely unexpected effect which you can catch and utilize.

Do you like to use multi-camera set-ups?

On big spectacular scenes I naturally film an enormous amount of material to cover. Otherwise I find myself tending to use fewer and fewer set-ups, though I doubt if I shall ever go so far as Godard's ten-minute takes, slowly panning from one spot to another, and back.

Are you able to work in complete independence?

Woodfall Films is a completely independent company, but this of course is dependent on our obtaining the backing we need from the distributors, and that in turn is dependent on the number of flops we have. As a rule we spend our own money on the early stages of developing a project, and then go to one of the big companies for finance. I find the American companies generally much freer and easier, much less likely to interfere with you. At the moment there is a recession in American interest over here, because all the most successful films recently have been American, which naturally tempts money back into their own studios; but this can change back again at any time.

4. The Actor
(Stars, Crowd and Stunt)

In feature films, it is still the name of the star, more even than that of the director, which counts at the box office. It is doubtful whether any director's name – with the possible exception of Hitchcock's – has by itself sufficient drawing power to fill a cinema. But how far is a film actor responsible for his or her performance?

Alec Guinness's comment, in an interview which follows (page 112), on the status of the film actor – that he is entirely in the hands of the director and technicians – is fundamental; obviously no director or editor in his senses would want to ruin a good performance deliberately, but the actor's fear that this can and does happen is a very real one. On the other hand, there is no doubt that a director, or even an editor, can create a 'star' out of a 'bad' actor who possessed (by traditional theatrical standards) minimal interpretative ability and whose only attribute is a photogenic screen presence. Because very often a film actor's success is absolutely and inseparably related to a specific film, and because even the star cannot be judged in isolation from everyone else involved in the making of a film, it is practically impossible to tell whether an actor's brilliant performance in a film is due to his own abilities, or due to the director's instructions or the editor's cutting. Many a 'good' actor has given a bad performance in a film, and, what is especially important, many a third-rate actor has been hailed as a genius. For these reasons the performance (and the ability to judge it) of a film actor in a film is very different from that of an actor in the theatre.

The power of editing to change the actual meaning read into an actor's expression was demonstrated years ago in a famous experiment by the Russian director Lev Kuleshov and his then pupil V. Pudovkin. Kuleshov followed a single, expressionless close-up of the actor Ivan Mosjoukine with three shots: (1) a plate of soup; (2) a coffin containing a woman's body; and (3) a little girl playing with a toy. Each shot was intercut with the original close-up of the actor's face. In his book *Film Technique and Film Acting* Pudovkin wrote of the result: 'The public raved about the acting of the artist. They pointed out the heavy pensiveness of his mood over the forgotten soup, were touched and moved by the deep sorrow with which he looked on the dead woman, and admired the light, happy smile with which he surveyed the girl at play. But we knew that in all three cases the face was exactly the same.' Alfred Hitchcock has also remarked on the transformations editing may produce in the way an actor is seen on the screen by an audience: 'Imagine James Stewart looking at a mother nursing a child. You see the child, then cut back to him. He smiles. Now Mr Stewart is a benign old gentleman. Take away the middle piece of film and substitute a shot of a girl in a bikini. *Now* he's a dirty old man.'

Some of the people I have interviewed comment on the film actor's special role in a film performance:

Fred Zinnemann (director): 'It [the alteration of the quality of a performance by manipulation in the cutting-room] is possible: it has been done many times, and I can sympathize with the actor's feelings in the matter.'

Lindsay Anderson (director): 'This is a very natural fear of the actor, often justified. His performance can be ruined by people he has never met, or who have never genuinely considered what he has been trying to do. But this is to consider a perversion of what ought to happen. If a performance is edited with skill, and at least with the director in constant attendance, then the cutting can make the most of it. In some ways editing is an advantage of the cinema over the theatre, in that you can select all the most successful and impressive moments and suppress the bad ones. It's true that if a director uses the right face at the right moment it's not necessary for a great deal of acting to go on. The audience will do the work themselves, when they see what the face is reacting to. I remember watching John Ford directing a jungle scene in a studio for *Mogambo* (1953) in which Donald Sinden was supposed to be frightened by a gorilla. No gorilla was there, of course, it had been shot on location and would be cut in afterwards. Ford told Sinden: "You don't have to look *too* terrified – the audience will be terrified for you." '

Gregory Peck (*actor*): 'Neither director nor editor can supply what isn't there. He can minimize the effect of a poor or an inept performance simply by staying off the performer and allowing his lines to be played on the face of a better actor. He can manipulate, but he cannot supply. Nothing can come out which has not been put in.'

Sidney Lumet (*director*): 'A performance *can* be altered, particularly in the editing. Also, the camera itself can fight what an actor is doing. It is easier to ruin a good performance in the cutting-room than to make a good one from a bad one. You may improve it, but that is as far as it can go. On the other hand, when there is a real *rapport* between director and actor, screen acting can be not only far from a "non-art" but one of the greatest expressions of the acting art. The illumination of a character as you build it up in a mosaic, as contrasted to continual development in the theatre, demands such technical skill that when it is successfully achieved I feel that something very major has been accomplished.'

Peter Hall (*director*): 'I believe that great film actors are great actors. It's true that the great film actor who has the courage and honesty to reveal himself totally to the camera, as he must, is often incapable of being a great stage actor, because he has not the technical dexterity to project his truth. Similarly, quite a lot of great stage actors are so dexterous at projecting their truth that all the camera sees is the projection, and not the truth. Great actors can be great in both media, but no actor can be made into a genius by the best director and editor in the world.'

Kevin Brownlow (editor): 'There's no doubt an editor can change a performance – or at least to some extent conceal a bad one. He can, for instance, choose the best shot, and the best track for an actor's delivery, and put the two together. He can also use longshots, or cut away from a poor actor.'

John Frankenheimer (director): 'A director *can* ruin a performance, though he can't make a great one out of a poor one – only cover it up a little. But let me put it this way: I think every director would like to have on film performances by actors of Alec Guinness's stature to fool around with in the cutting-room!'

Apart from his vulnerability in the hands of the editor, an actor may also on occasion have to project his performance through elaborate make-up which may have taken anything up to four hours (or longer) to prepare. The searching proximity of the camera makes such disguises a work of much greater complexity and precision than is usually the case in the theatre, and make-up is not left to the artist himself to apply. Horror and science-fiction characters such as Frankenstein's monster, wolf-men, or other-planet aliens, as might be expected, generally call for the most elaborate effects. On occasion a transformation from man into beast, for instance, may be so complete that the genuine is almost indistinguishable from the fake, as in *2001: A Space Odyssey* (1966, directed by Stanley Kubrick), or it may result in an extremely skilful blending of human with animal, as in *Planet of the Apes* (1967, directed by Franklin Schaffner). (See illustration 23.)

In the following pages four actors and two actresses discuss aspects of their work in feature films.

James Mason

'I regard film as an important branch of current literature, a reflection of the thought and history of our day, whether drama or comedy. Films should be completely modern, with the freshness of last week's magazine or yesterday's newspaper. My own choice of scripts is, of course, limited to those submitted to me by a producer or director, as I am not strong enough in the industry to set up, or get backing for, projects of my own. In earlier days my aim was always to find a script in which it would be possible to put over joy and excitement on the screen. Nowadays I would to some extent qualify that, but I still like to work on something which enables me to communicate an element of joy.'

Do you put in much preliminary work on a character before shooting starts?

Unless I'm taking an authoritative part, as for instance in *Age of Consent* with Michael Powell, when I got together with the director and we did a lot of creative work together on the script, I do most of my preparation by myself. In the case of a historical character, such as *Rommel, Desert Fox* (1951) or Franz-Joseph in *Mayerling* (1968), it's simply a question of reading up everything which can be found about them and the period in which they lived. What makes movie acting difficult in relation to the theatre is that really you have to do your own homework – not only before the film starts but day by day as it is being shot. You must be a complete master of all the mechanical necessities of the part you play: the exact manner in which the character moves, speaks, behaves. Some actors carry it even further than that, and do not even rely on other actors to help them along the way. Marlon Brando, for instance, is quoted as saying that when he is playing opposite another actor he has no need to draw anything at all from him. When an actor is speaking in close-up, the character being spoken to is usually requested to answer with his own lines, standing eye-to-eye with him. Brando would rather look into space, and use his own imagination to feed him. I, on the contrary, like to receive whatever is available from the actors around me: I find the personal exchange very often of the greatest possible help. In *The Seagull* (1969), for instance, not only did I receive the most wonderful assistance from Vanessa Redgrave's speaking of her lines and from the way she reacted to mine, but also she was entirely unpredictable herself, constantly expressing thoughts with her eyes or her manner of speaking to which I could react in an altogether fresh way myself.

Do you notice much difference in film-playing technique during the years you have been working in the cinema?

Yes, an enormous difference. When I started in England in 1935, in rather cheap pictures, everything was rather crude, cut to the basic long-shot, medium-shot, close-shot. Nothing was performed at great length, and actors were not required to carry long continuous scenes for many minutes at a time. I think Orson Welles in *Citizen Kane* (1941) was the first person to play scenes of four or five minutes at a stretch. Even after this, the method in Hollywood remained very much the same until the more recent liberation came from the postwar films, principally of Italy, France and England.

The German director, F.W. Murnau, used to say to his actors: 'Don't act, think!' Would you agree with this?

Yes, it is, of course, basic, though a little misleading as true acting *is* thinking, is behaving. Many actors are at a loss when they are not actually speaking lines. In my opinion lines are merely a decoration to the scenes taking place. You are acting because you are behaving as the character you create would behave in a given set of circumstances. Very often a scene would be just as effective without the words written for it; in fact it's frequently from habit that actors are supplied with too many words, too much dialogue.

Do you also agree with the saying that it is impossible to lie to the camera?

I'd say it is very *possible* to lie. Television has proved this: you have only to think of salesmen in commercials, or politicians making speeches, to realize this.

Does the lack of continuity in film acting worry you?

It's obviously true that the nearer you can approximate to shooting in continuity the easier everything becomes – but it's

not essential, and with practice it becomes quite simple provided you do enough preparation to have the whole character in
mind.

*Do you like to improvise, and does the opportunity often
occur?*

Yes, I do – and no, it doesn't. The film in which I was able to
improvise the most was Stanley Kubrick's *Lolita* (1962). We did
this strictly at rehearsal level, to explore and get intimately
acquainted with the significance of various scenes. Kubrick first
hit upon the idea because he became aware of the fact that Sue
Lyon, who played Lolita, knew the script back to front, and
front to back, but really needed to be induced to think of the
lines in a particular scene as something that came out of the
feeling of the character in that scene. So we started improvis-
ing during rehearsals – forgot the lines we'd learned and got to
grips with the situation instead, finding that this helped us to
understand much more quickly what each scene was basically
about. Sue Lyon made a considerable contribution to many of
the scenes because she spoke the same language as the character
she was playing. This opportunity doesn't often occur, however,
mainly owing to the stringency of the budget – and there are
many film writers and producers to whom improvisation is a
dirty word.

*Do you prefer working on location, or in the studio where
conditions are more controlled?*

In theory I like the 'true backgrounds' of location, but the
technical difficulties are such that actors often find themselves
more inhibited than when making-believe in studio conditions.
This applies specially to interiors. A real room doesn't seem like
a real room anyway, because it will be cluttered to the ceiling
with all kinds of apparatus, and the heat of the lights is ap-
palling. The physical obstacles are worse than those you en-
counter in a studio without the compensating advantage of true
reality.

Do you find post-synchronizing a burden?

No, because I find it easy to recall all the experience of creating a character, and I'm often very glad of the process because the conditions on location are often not good. I may be

dissatisfied with my voice on hearing it afterwards, particularly if I've been using a special type of speech or accent, and perhaps have not really mastered it at the time of shooting.

Have you ever directed a film in which you have also played? What are your views on this?

I directed myself in one or two stage productions many years ago, and in a few television shorts, but never in a feature film. I've always wanted to direct; partly because I love movies and want to be more and more creatively involved in them, partly because it often happens that I feel I could contribute a good deal more than the official director of the film. At the same time I've always accepted a strong discipline in movie-making: there are many different ways of directing any particular scene and no ultimately perfect way, and obviously a film should not be directed by a committee with each individual involved discussing over and over what he considers the approach should be. Provided a director has a good record and is accepted by the qualified technicians and actors around him, he should be allowed the final authority. I think that to direct oneself as an actor is extremely difficult and has seldom been done successfully. If you quote, say, Olivier's *Hamlet* to me, I would reply: yes, wonderful, but I have just a slight suspicion that his performance as an actor might have been that tiny amount greater if he had been able to relax and concentrate entirely on this. *Citizen Kane*? That worked fine, but I would say that Orson Welles is an artist who is able to act with the top of his mind, without being as deeply involved as some other actors – that he can concentrate with 20 per cent of his mind as an actor, leaving a lively 80 per cent for his job as a director.

Jill Bennett

'I don't think acting is an art, because it is an interpretative act rather than a creative one. The director is an artist, the writer certainly most of all, but the actor is an interpreter of what he or she is given. This applies to both stage and screen. The two forms are basically the same for the actor – a search for the truth. Personally, I like the discipline of film acting: in the theatre you are on your own, but on the set the director is boss. Actresses seem to find it easier to submit to this necessary total obedience than actors – the feminine temperament perhaps! It doesn't worry me that the film is regarded as the director's medium. In the theatre you act to the audience, on the set you act to the director and your audience is the camera crew. This makes me nervous sometimes, but not self-conscious: in films everyone is a specialist, and you are there with your particular craft to deliver your share of the goods. There's a lot of boredom attached to it – hours of waiting while lights and cameras are set up – but in the end it's rewarding because you can get more depth into your characterization than you can in the theatre. You can't lie to the camera in the way you can behind the protective proscenium arch of the stage.

'I prefer rehearsing to playing in the theatre, and loathe long runs – in the cinema you never have time to get stale. The reason I prefer location is that it's away from any suggestion of the theatre, and I find the variety and "danger" of location work stimulating. I like the *ad hoc* business of filming. For my long scene in the tent with Lord Cardigan in *The Charge of the Light Brigade* (1968), we had one rehearsal, then went straight into it – one take, then close-ups, with things being changed right up to the last minute. You have to get used to it, but it's exciting.

'I make careful notes to overcome the lack of continuity, and this does not worry me very much. But post-synching is ghastly. The whole of my lengthy heart attack in *The Nanny* (1965, directed by Seth Holt) was post-synchronized – all that gasping and groaning. It's almost impossible not to change your performance, if only because your *face* is different, and you also come across unexpected cuts.

'Ideally, an actress should work in all three media, theatre, film and television. You can learn something from each which can be of help in the others, and although the techniques are different, they should not be looked on as mutually exclusive.'

Gregory Peck

'I think the best way to define "star quality" is to look at the "stayers" among the big Hollywood names, such as Bogart, Tracy, Cooper, Cagney. It's very interesting to watch the old Bogart films they're showing now on television. You see a fellow quite unlike the full-blown Bogart – a tentative fellow, unsure of himself, not nearly as well developed, as exciting, as rounded a personality as the man you see when he has come into his own, found himself, achieved his true poise, become whole, so to speak. You'll find the same progression with any of the great stars. What you watch through a succession of roles is a maturing process, and the only people who reached and retained the star stature are the people who grew and changed, became richer in their outlook and more interesting people in themselves. You get the sense of a developing and deepening personality through what they have been able to bring to each role and situation. I came to films from the theatre, and while I love the theatre and have the greatest respect for an accomplished stage performance, I think one must admit that there's a great deal in the theatre to help the actor along. For example, he is more likely to be dealing with material of some literary merit than in the cinema, and this makes acting easier. The audience is there present, and the fact of doing the play in continuity means that he has the lift of that audience's expectation, and is the focus of their attention. His adrenalin comes up to meet the challenge. There is the advantage of the build-up – before he reaches the crisis scenes the building blocks are slowly laid in place, and the character develops so that he can get a great momentum going. We don't have any of those advantages on the screen. We have to supply our own audience. Very often we're dealing with material which is no more than popular fiction, and somehow, by force of concentration or strength of personality, we have to make it appear better than it is. You might say that star quality is the power to make popular fiction look like something much better.

'The new techniques of film-making are stimulating to a point, but they are sometimes used as a crutch, or an easy superficial way of keeping the screen moving and visually active to try to conceal the emptiness behind them. Over-used, they become simply sophomoric – a young director playing with a new toy. And in actual fact, of course, very little is new – nearly everything that can be done with the camera has been done before – though technical inventions, in lenses for instance, are continually being developed. Idea, content, perceptiveness, depth of emotion, the human qualities – these are the true basis of the cinema. Modern techniques and ingenious new methods are only valuable in so far as they contribute to these qualities.'

Sandy Dennis

'Playing in the theatre is something I long for – I never long for films. I even prefer working in the studio to location because it approximates to the theatre. I find looping (post-synchronizing) very difficult, probably because I don't have a musical ear and so I'm not able to listen to the *sound* of what I said before and repeat it as if it was music, which is a very necessary part of post-synchronizing. On the other hand, playing a part out of continuity doesn't worry me in the least – perhaps it would be better for me if it did!

'I don't find it necessary as a rule to do a lot of preliminary work with a director on building up a character. Obviously if a director asks you to try something, you try it, even if you think it's wrong (after all, it may be you who's wrong!), but in the ordinary way I don't need to ask him for very much. I like to be given straightforward, simple directions such as "Do that a little faster, or a little slower," not "You do this because you are feeling sad," I know I'm supposed to be feeling sad. I want to be told the result, not how to arrive at it. The reason I so liked working with Mike Nichols in *Who's Afraid of Virginia Woolf?* (1966) was that he approached so many points through humour. He also gave line readings, which is unusual and which many actors hate, but he has such a wonderful sense of timing that he could give me the result he wanted by reading the words. Above all, he gave me the greatest gift which it lies in a director's power to give an actor he trusts – the ability to go much too far, to be foolish in fact. Where a lot of directors would say, "No, no, we could never use that," he would deliberately encourage an actor to try it. That suited me, because I know people are either tremendously offended by me, or like what I do. I feel I haven't yet learned enough to lose myself in the portrayal of a character. I still use a lot of my own personality. I would like one day to be able to do something in which there is nothing of *me*.

'And it's not true that you can't lie to the camera. You can. I do it all the time. I always have other things on my mind!'

Richard Attenborough

'From the actor's point of view cinema and theatre are as far apart as chalk and cheese – any comparison can only be between opposites. The most evident contrast is that in the theatre your prime responsibility is to be seen and heard from the front row of the stalls to the back row of the gallery, which means projection of voice, personality, expression, emotion. In the cinema the antithesis is required. *Any* projection becomes unreal. Theatricality is the one adjective least applicable to the film. You have to be constantly aware that within two feet of you is an EYE, and within six inches an EAR. Consequently any slight doubt in thought, any lack of clarity in decision is immediately apparent.

'In addition, cinema acting is bound up with the sort of technique which demands, for instance, hitting marks on the floor, taking up a position in terms of lights, avoiding plunging the person you're talking to into shadow, making sure that if you bend down to pick something up from the floor you do so with sufficient precision of timing to allow the cameraman to know when you go down and when you come up. All this requires a tremendous knowledge of the problems of technique, and a colossal power of concentration. By the first day you walk on to a film set you must have both the overall characterization and any problems of technique so firmly in your mind that you can put them into the background; and your whole attention can then be concentrated on the manner of behaviour of your particular character in the particular scene that is being filmed. For example, if you've got to weep at your daughter's wedding, you've got to think about what it's like to weep at your daughter's wedding: if you've also got to think about the particular sort of man who's going to weep, then you've left it too late.

- 'In my early days in films I found the lack of continuity in shooting very confusing – meeting my wife for the first time weeks after I'd already made love to her, or grieving over the death of a friend before I even knew who was playing him – I found this difficult. You have to know the script through and through before going on the floor. Robert Donat used to have a sort of temperature or stock-and-share graph right across the wall of his dressing-room on which he set out all the scenes in which his character appeared and drew lines in different colours signifying his age, emotional climate, relationship with the other characters, and so on, in each instance. I don't really like improvisation, because the essence of any art form is precision and control of materials. And as for post-synchronizing, the mesmerizing effect of those wretched lines as they move across the screen destroys a performance. It's a diabolical process!'

Alec Guinness

'I don't think the actor has the status of an artist in the film world for the simple reason that he has not the final say about the selection, so to speak, of his performance. In one film, for instance, a comedy, there was a very big laugh at the beginning which I knew I should then kill, not encouraging any more laughter for a short time. When the film was finally cut they took the beginning and put it at the end. Well, that sort of thing makes nonsense of an actor's performance. In the theatre, if you have to make a cut you will adjust accordingly. If the cut contains something important from the point of view of character development you can remould it, insert it into another part of the play. Unless a film is re-shot you can't do this. Film-making is enjoyable, but it's the director's medium. As an actor you are entirely in the hands of the technicians. They certainly know their job, but it's not the same job. The lack of continuity is another point: when you play the final or the central scenes of a film before the early ones you're really just guessing in the dark as to how far you can go emotionally, though a first-class director is of course a very good judge of this. For this reason I like to rehearse as much as possible beforehand. I also prefer working in the controlled conditions of the studio to going on location. So often you have to rush things through because of weather conditions, or you have to sit around pretending it's sunny when it's freezing or vice versa. In *Dr Zhivago* (1965), we were all in Madrid, in a temperature of 116 degrees, muffled up to our ears in furs. All you can think of is – let's say the lines and get out of this heat!

'An aspect of film acting which is preferable to the theatre is that you don't have to face the wearying possibility of a long run. If you are working in a good film there will be some part of each day – even if it is only a minute or so – which is fresh and challenging. The most exciting part of the theatre to me is the rehearsal period, the creative period. In filming, every day may provide some little scene in which your antennae have got to be out because it is a little moment of genuinely creative work.'

Crowd and stunt artists

In Britain the term 'extra' is going out of use, although it is still customary in the United States where they are represented by the Screen Extras Guild. The equivalent British union is the Film Artistes' Association, to which all crowd artists must belong. Basically the conditions of work are the same in London and in Hollywood, in that practically all casting for crowd work is done through a central agency; in London the agency is Central Casting Limited.

Crowd artists keep in touch with Central Casting by telephone each day if they are available for work, and the production companies notify their requirements to Central Casting in the evening for the next morning. The volume of casting requirements varies widely each night: one evening a single production may need between 700 and 800 people; the following day all the companies put together may ask for less than 100. Anything may be demanded at short notice. For *The Most Dangerous Man in the World* (1969, directed by J. Lee-Thompson) for instance, the agency was asked to supply 250 Chinese, and managed to do so.

Central Casting also caters for stunt men, but in both Britain and America there are separate agencies for this specialized work, such as the aptly named Tough Guys Agency in London, run by Reuben Martin and Wallace Schulberg. Wallace Schulberg describes their work:

'We have about one hundred men and half a dozen girls. A film company will ring up and say "We want a bald fat man to jump out of a seventy-foot high building, or a short hairy one to drive a car through a plate-glass window" – and we'll have no difficulty in finding both of them. Our age range is from about eighteen to sixty – one stunt man in his sixties still does excellent falls. Many members specialize in some particular stunt. A lot of the fight work is done on the trampoline: you see someone flung high into the air across a saloon bar and through a window, he starts it from a trampoline out of camera range. That takes a lot of practice. Furniture to be smashed is generally either made of balsa wood or pre-sawn, and glass is made of rosin. I myself did one job where I had to dive through a pub window. It was successful, but I had to do it ten times before the cameraman was satisfied. Naturally, a director uses as few takes as he can for stunts, but it's always possible that a man might have to crash a car three or four times before it can be passed.

'The general idea of a stunt man is somebody very big and tough, but often they are just the opposite, and this is very necessary. A director might want, say, a foreign diplomat to fall down a flight of stairs. Sometimes, too, we need men who can put on women's clothes and a wig to take some of the rough stuff for her. Our half a dozen girls are capable of doing most things themselves, particularly tumbling, handsprings, back somersaults. A girl, being more supple than a man, is able to take a hard blow and make it look good. But they also crash cars, fall off horses and jump from roofs. A lot of stunt work is, of course, doubling for stars, very few of whom would be permitted, even if they were able, to risk life and limb and the money involved. The famous car chase in *Bullitt* (1968, directed by Peter Yates), where Steve McQueen did all his own driving, is exceptional. In a series like the Bond films every stunt man in the country might be called.

'Stunt men are not entitled to any insurance in the event of accident. They have to sign a form with the film company declaring that all stunts are undertaken at the artist's own risk. Minor accidents occur constantly, serious ones occasionally. Stunt men have been killed, but this is extremely rare, considering the risks they have to take despite all precautions.'

To give some idea of what is involved in a spectacular crash, Jack Cardiff describes in detail the death of the *Girl on a Motorcycle*, which he directed in 1968, and in which, incidentally, Marianne Faithfull's riding had been doubled throughout by a slim be-wigged young man.

'A team of motoring experts who specialize in crashes was consulted, and I explained that we wanted a truck to move into the centre of the road, the motorcycle to hit the front wheel, and the girl rider to crash head first into the windscreen of a car which was then rammed by another car. It was done, of course, in a number of separate cuts, but the really tricky part was obviously the motorcyclist hitting the truck wheel and going through the windscreen. Our young double got on a duplicate motorcycle, drove it up to thirty miles an hour, and did just what he appeared to do – ran straight into the truck and somersault through the air. You may imagine my feelings as I watched him do it! This was intercut with shots of the real girl. For the dive into the windscreen we had the Triplex glass people prepare a special sheet of extremely thin material into which she (he) could dive quite safely. Then we had to arrange for the second car to approach from behind, run into the back of the first car and go right over it. To achieve this (at an actual speed of 30 m.p.h. photographed to appear at an apparent speed of 80 m.p.h.) the crash experts fastened an H-type girder on to the back of the first car out of range of the camera, so that it became a sort of ramp. The stunt man then drove at this, got his wheel right into the girder, and this caused him to go up over the car in front of him and at the same time turn over in the air. He managed the whole effect perfectly at the first attempt. The entire episode was photographed with the three cameras, one of which was strapped into the car which turned over. Everything went without a hitch, but I would not like to have had to take it a second time!'

5. The Cameraman

The lighting cameraman, or director of photography, is responsible for the shooting of the entire film, but he does not handle the camera himself: this is the job of the camera operator. In earlier years the two were combined, but as equipment became more sophisticated it was found necessary to divide the work, and the lighting cameraman now concentrates more on lighting and setting-up for angles (in conjunction with the director and camera operator), and less on standing by the camera. He uses the camera, as Douglas Slocombe says, 'as a mental reference for the picture which he tries to create with light – and this is why he is called the lighting cameraman. Nowadays "director of photography" is becoming the more usual name.'

His team consists of the camera operator, the focus puller, the camera grip and the clapper-boy. The latter marks the beginning of each take visually (by holding up a board on which its reference number is chalked) and aurally (by snapping a hinged wooden strip down on the board, the crack registering on the sound track). This dual operation enables the sound and picture tracks to be 'married' accurately in the cutting-room when the film is edited. The clapper-boy is also responsible for loading the film into the camera magazine, and for the gear as a whole. The camera operator is the man who actually manipulates the camera, but he is also responsible for such matters as the actual working out of camera angles in accordance with the instructions of the director. The focus puller keeps the moving camera in focus, working out the various depths and controlling the zoom lens.

A recent occasional addition to the team is a helicopter pilot. Helicopters are being used more and more frequently for scenes which a short while ago would have been taken from a camera crane. Although the method is very costly, it enables a cameraman to secure practically any effect he wants. A helicopter with a zoom lens, for instance, can, in a single shot and keeping rock steady, start with an extreme close-up of a girl looking out of a train window, and end up with a distant view of the train running across a viaduct.

A lighting cameraman is engaged by the producer for a particular film. He works in the closest collaboration with the director during the period of shooting. He is one of the earliest members of the unit to be called in at the start of a project, once the financial preparations have been completed.

In the following pages, four leading cameramen talk about their work.

Douglas Slocombe

'It's with interiors that the lighting cameraman really comes into his own, and his imagination has full play. He can create his own picture. In location work you're in the hands of the elements, and have to adapt. For this reason it's essential that you should have a strong hand in selecting locations – and also the opportunity to visit them beforehand. This is not possible as often as it might be expected to be, and as it ought to be. During the making of *The Italian Job* (1969, director Peter Collinson), I went to a location I hadn't seen before and found it was on the wrong side of a mountain, where the sun never shone. We had to cart the entire production, unit and equipment, over to the other side. Matching shots from different locations can present problems, too. *Boom* (1968, director Joseph Losey) was very tricky in this respect. We built expensive exteriors and interiors on a cliff-top in Sardinia and also shot the interiors in studios in Rome. We had the extremely strong Sardinian sunlight reflected from the pure white façades, then went immediately to rooms lit only by high arc-lights, and afterwards had to combine movements from one to the other. It was like trying to link up candlelight with the sun.

'The procedures adopted for night shooting are governed by the type of setting. With an open landscape any attempt at artificial lighting would look unnatural, so I generally film in the daytime using special filters combined with controlled underexposure. Nearly all Westerns are shot this way, but in England there is a sky problem – so much of the time it's grey! When night shooting in a street, or any background with artificial lighting, this principle of course does not apply – nor does it invariably apply in open country. In *Robbery,* for instance, all the train attack sequences were shot at night.

'We have little choice nowadays as to whether or not we photograph in colour. Personally, I regret the almost total passing of black-and-white, though I admit that now the first frenzy has passed and techniques have improved, colour can be used very dramatically. Restraint is the keyword. I was able to conjure up the cold, dank, gloomy atmosphere of a twelfth-century castle for *The Lion in Winter* (1968, director Anthony Harvey) far more satisfactorily than I should have been able to do in black-and-white, even in the daytime. I carefully avoided any "pure" colour here – it would have been an intrusion. I tried to let tints glow through palely. The secret is to photograph places and objects *less* colourfully than they would appear in real life. On the other hand, there are many old black-and-white films which had no need of it. I think *The Servant* (1963, director Joseph Losey), which was in black-and-white, would have lost rather than gained by the addition of colour.

'I felt much the same hesitation on the arrival of Cinema-Scope. It takes time to get used to these things. With wide screens, the eye at close quarters cannot take in the whole scene, so important pieces of action have to be kept either towards the centre or close to the part where the last movement took place.

For close-ups I like to shade the sides, rather like using a mask – in the early days everyone seemed to be lying down! I hope that one day somebody will invent Super-Panavision – one big wide screen on top of another. Everybody will cry out how marvellous it is, until they realize they are back to the old original shape.

'Whatever the shape or size of the screen I prefer not to use many cameras except for stuntwork or big spectacles. For one thing, there is so much to exclude – tracks, booms, lights, other cameras, the continuity girl and crew – that you are merely multiplying your difficulties. More importantly, there can be only one camera angle for any one shot which is ideally lit. Camera trickery nowadays is more often than not laboratory trickery, which is less expensive and less risky. In *Kind Hearts and Coronets*, in 1949, it took us three days to make the famous shot of eight Alec Guinnesses sitting together in church; the camera had to be locked for three hours for each change of make-up. Nowadays we should simply take separate shots and put them all together in the laboratory. This sort of post-shooting manipulation has been developed into an art in itself, and is a great money saver. Stars can be so expensive that everybody is anxious to get rid of them as soon as possible. Nowadays we can say: "No matter what background they're supposed to be against – shoot them! We can easily fit the scenery in afterwards." I recently worked on a film which was actually in rough-cut when the producer decided that a certain piece of action didn't work at all well. He hit on the idea of literally substituting one actress for another at a key point. The change-over was effected entirely in the laboratory, without the use of any actresses at all. It's not improbable that in time whole films may be made, big casts and all, without anyone meeting anyone!

'There are, of course, other kinds of trickery – perhaps cunning would be a better word – more exclusively concerned with the camera itself, such as suggestion or distortion by the choice of angles. In *The Servant* we took a series of shots of the girl (Sarah Miles) lying in a revolving armchair with the young man she was seducing. Although she was in fact wearing a short jacket we were able, through the choice of camera angles on her legs, to suggest that she was completely naked. The firm which made the chair afterwards sold the model by the million!'[1]

Walter Lassally

'I believe in making use of any photographic process provided it suits the purpose of the moment, and is not merely brought in for effect. At present the fade and the dissolve are out of fashion, but if a situation would benefit from either I should not hesitate to use them. The danger with any new technique is that it will be used simply because it *is* new, something different. I like the hand-held camera, but at the moment it is being sadly overworked. I used it very early on in feature films, in *A Taste of Honey* (1961, director Tony Richardson), and in the documentary *We Are the Lambeth Boys* we made some of the first hand-held dialogue sequences; but like all novelties it can be abused. When CinemaScope first came out the same thing happened, it was used for totally unsuitable subjects. Some directors mastered it quickly – Truffaut, for instance, always used it magnificently: the point is that when it *is* well used, you should not even notice whether a film is in CinemaScope or not. I dislike the "wide-screen" shape intensely – it seems to me to make the worst of both worlds. The pressure is now on for a return to the old original screen shape, because it approximates that of the television screen. It is also the most satisfying aesthetically – the Greek "golden mean".

'Television may be responsible for a return to the old screen proportions, which is in its favour – but it is also responsible for the virtual disappearance of black-and-white, which is very much the opposite. The film-maker should be free to choose, because it is ruinous to certain subjects if they have to be made in colour. However subtly it is used, everything is apt to be over-dramatized, and to end up looking like a picture-postcard. We are still looking for an ideal process for night-shooting in colour. At present a great deal of "day-for-night" photography

1. This series of shots is reproduced in Alexander Walker's *Sex in the Movies*, Michael Joseph, 1966, Penguin Books, 1968.

is derived from the non-naturalistic stage effect – a blue bias. Real night is monochromatic. The nearest approach is obtained by tinted black-and-white. I tried out a new technique with filters in *The Day the Fish Came Out* (1967, director Michael Cacoyannis), but it was not entirely successful. The effect should be monochromatic until someone comes close to the camera, and no filter as yet can do this.

'In daytime shooting the main colour problem is that the light is constantly changing as the day goes by, and you can't leave things until the next morning because then the direction would be reversed. Not only is the light changing, but also the appearance of the sky itself, particularly with clouds around. However, thankfully, you can often get away with quite a lot! In addition, of course, you can supplement or manipulate natural light to some extent. This is not so much improving on nature as rendering it closer to what the human eye sees. The eye adjusts to a dark area, the lens does not, or at any rate it is unable to compensate extremes of light and darkness *in the same frame*.

'When you come down to it, however, most of the problems nowadays are human ones, not technical. All the technical problems have been faced before, but there are always human beings. One of the most essential qualifications for a lighting cameraman to possess is a sound knowledge of human psychology, because it is as important for him as for anyone else on the set to be able to reassure the actors and actresses with whom he is working. Many of them are very insecure people – and if they're not with you, there can be trouble!'

Jack Cardiff

'The lighting cameraman is basically the servant of the director. If a modern young director wants things flat and ugly, the cameraman must do just that. I was always interested in the dramatic side, and never felt I knew a great deal about optics. I used to hate being praised for "beautiful photography", with no dramatic creation behind it. I always wanted, in fact, to become a director.

'The hallmark of simple lighting is Rembrandt – light/dark/light/dark. I thank God the school is nearly extinct which taught people to use light all over the place. Spot-rails round the set are the cause of this unnatural spread from all sides – it totally destroys realism. Everything is, of course, much easier nowadays. When I was photographing *Black Narcissus* (1946, directed by Michael Powell and Emeric Pressburger), the key light on an actor's face had to equal over 1,000 candlepower, now we need only 80. Up to a certain point you always have to have white light on colour. In the early days we used white arc-lamps – for *Black Narcissus*, *The Red Shoes* (1948, directed by Powell and Pressburger), and even *War and Peace* (1956, directed by King Vidor), it was entirely arc-lamps. Then Eastmancolour brought out film which could be used with incandescent light uncorrected, the corrections being made later in the laboratories. This was a great break-through. Nowadays, in a dim scene, you can use just one small lamp which you can carry in your hand, without any necessity for covering lights. There was also the nuisance of huge blimps – padded surrounds to render the camera soundproof. In the early days of sound these were like small bungalows – now they are tiny. The BMC Mitchell is in itself a little blimp. All this, together with the smaller cameras, means an enormous increase in freedom for all of us, including the actors who can move around as they feel, to a far greater extent than hitherto.

'An ever-present problem is that of reflection off polished surfaces, spectacles, car bodies, windows. I always experience a sinking feeling when an actor says, "I think it would be great if I wore glasses!" Cars are often sprayed to avoid flares (though an occasional flare can be effective); pictures can be tilted from the wall; and in the case of windows I sometimes have each pane taken out and angled by the insertion of nails in the frame. Removing the glass altogether always looks wrong, and the same applies to spectacles – since Harold Lloyd! But it's a constant problem, and generally impossible to solve completely.

'Colour should never be compulsory. A film like *Sons and Lovers*, which I directed in 1960 (photographed by Freddie Francis), would have lost all its gritty, grimy, coal-pit atmosphere if we had been forced to make it in colour. It is almost impossible to achieve *drabness* in a colour film.

'Even in the black-and-white days I "improved on nature", mainly by the use of filters, to make the sky darker and sharpen contrasts. I used dark red or infra-red filters for night shots. In addition we had graduated filters, of varying densities from top to bottom. I think I was one of the very first cameramen to use *colour* graduated filters. These will enable a scene which is too bright in the upper or lower part of the view (a glaringly hot desert, for instance) to be modified at will by moving or reversing the filter. These for years were made by a little old lady living in a tiny country cottage overflowing with cats. She made them in a kind of magic brew – an air of mystery and magic, in fact, surrounded her altogether. She was a legendary figure, regarded as the greatest maker of colour filters in Britain – if not in the world.

'Here are two examples of improving on nature. Some years ago I was on top of Mount Vesuvius, filming an actual eruption of the volcano – which meant lugging one of the old, heavy cameras up the side of the mountain. The lava was exceedingly hot, and dropping all around us in a highly uncomfortable manner. But it wasn't behaving at all dramatically in the camera. We decided to make it come out more quickly, so we shot it at about six instead of the usual twenty-four frames per second. Its colour didn't come out very well either, so we didn't equalize the change in exposure by shutting down the lens diaphragm. This meant that the lava was very over-exposed. The joint result was an explosion on the screen of fast-moving, bright red, menacing lava, instead of the sluggish, dull-coloured stuff it naturally was. In *Western Approaches*, during the war, I needed a close-up to fit in with a previous scene which had been shot in the sunshine. This looked impossible, as we were at sea, with a dark, dirty grey sky. So I used an incandescent orange-yellow light, without the usual blue filter to correct it, over-exposed it deliberately to bring out the sky a pure white, and gave instructions for it to be printed with ten points of blue. The final picture looked exactly like the sunrise at the start of a perfect, blue-skied summer day. Of course, sometimes such interferences backfire. In *Scott of the Antarctic* (1948, directed by Charles Frend), we had to film a scene which was supposed to take place in a green tent. Obviously, there was no room to shoot actually inside the tent, so we shot against parts of it as a background, with green filters to make it appear that the actors were really inside. The following day we had a telephone call from the laboratories – they were very sorry that they were unable to send the rushes, as something had gone very wrong. But we were not to worry, it was being investigated. Time went by, and we began to feel anxious. After several days the rushes turned up, with profuse apologies for the delay. The unaccountable trouble had been put right. When we ran the film, we found everything completely restored to "normal" – no vestige of green remained – nobody in the lab could believe that our mistake was deliberate.'

Oswald Morris

'Normally I prefer to work on a single-camera system. In shooting duologue scenes for instance, I always film the sequence twice rather than use two "over-shoulder" cameras. Even if you can get both characters perfectly lit, it is impossible to approach the eye-lines without recording the other camera. This means that you are removed by quite a wide angle from the direction in which each player is looking, which considerably weakens the scene, in addition to losing any feeling of intimacy. The disadvantages of shooting the entire scene twice is that the film may not be perfectly cut together, resulting in slight differences of expression on an actor's face as he appears in the merged alternating shots. Nowadays the zoom lens will be used more and more in such circumstances, but this still needs perfecting.

'The whole of *The Taming of the Shrew* (1967, directed by Franco Zeffirelli) was shot in the studio. Richard Burton and Elizabeth Taylor never went outside. We did it all with filters on lamps and cameras. Much of *Moulin Rouge* (1953, directed by John Huston) was photographed in a studio full of fog: we used vaporized oil to get the hazy atmosphere of the period,

The whole place was thick with it every morning – very unpleasant. Owing to the bad working conditions we had to give the electricians extra milk. An innovation in *Moby Dick* (1956, directed by Huston) was the overlaying of the three colour negatives with a fourth, a grey image to give the whole film the appearance of an old aquatint. This was the first time such a process had been tried. A similar experiment was made in Huston's *Reflections in a Golden Eye* (1967) to achieve a kind of washed-out gold effect, but this has not been publicly shown. The pressure of the commercial boys always comes down on innovations!'

6. The Art Director

The art director, or production designer, is creatively responsible to the director for everything seen on the screen around the actors. If the cameraman is the right hand of the director, the art director is the left, but neither cameraman nor director can function until the designer has produced the visual setting and style of the film. They work very closely as a creative team, the team being headed by the director, but the designer is also very closely linked with the producer to achieve the visual style; he has to design sets, estimate their cost, and calculate the studio space required for the film as a whole. With the producer, director, and cameraman, he is involved in selecting locations, and it is he who designs the overall relationship of locations to studio sets, or of outdoor location to interior location in actual buildings. Great ingenuity can be shown in this respect from the financial aspect. In Karel Reisz's *Isadora* (1969), for example, a single mansion near London served during two weeks of filming as ten different locations, exterior and interior, in scenes representing Moscow, Paris, Berlin, New York, Chicago, Boston and London. Conversely, in Lindsay Anderson's *If ...* (1968), four different college locations, interior and exterior, and several studio sets were smoothly put together and blended into one fictional school building.

The art director has under him one of the largest units in the studios. The art department comprises, besides draughtsmen, the assistant art director, a set dresser or decorator (responsible for providing the sets with, for example, furniture, curtains, chandeliers, ornaments) and a buyer who buys the props. Implementing the working drawings are plumbers, carpenters, plasterers, tinsmiths, property makers, scenic artists, and painters. The contact between the designer and these departments is through a construction manager, who functions in the same way as a 'clerk of works' functions with an architect. On some elaborate films, where set-up sketches are needed, there will be a sketch artist working with the designer and the director. His job is to put down in sketch form the various cuts that together comprise a sequence, for example a difficult non-dialogue action sequence or a musical dance sequence. From these sketches, which strung together look like a very large cartoon, the final plan of shooting can be agreed upon, thus saving possible wastage.

John Box comments on his work as production designer:

'Designing is not just sets. It is, in fact, not a set you're putting there, it's an image. And to get that image you must start by firstly thinking very carefully of the character, what he is doing, what he is feeling and thinking, and then arranging the setting, studio or location, around him.

'What the designer should consider is the mood and atmosphere in relation to the role. What effect do we want round this person, and how do we achieve it? There must be nothing arbitrary about the background. *That* must be the place where *this* person is at *this* time – and the audience must be convinced of its inevitability. The designer must not be self-indulgent, his background must never distract from the character in the foreground. In fact, if he's done his job properly the audience should never notice that he's been at work.

'In *A Man for All Seasons* (1967) nothing was put in a set unless it was functional. Not a chair was placed in a room unless it was sat on. I was not principally interested in the architecture, but in the atmosphere and the habits of the people of the period. Take that early scene where Wolsey is confronted by Thomas More. Fred Zinnemann's intention was to present Wolsey as power and authority. That, to me, meant a feeling of claustrophobia which would accentuate the character and power of Wolsey, and would involve the audience with Thomas More as he was confronted by the great man of the time. So we put Wolsey in a small room to emphasize his largeness. He wears red robes, so we don't want any other colours to lead your eye away from the central figure, so the walls become a darker shade of the same red. There are no corners in the room. The table at which he sits is smaller than it would have been in reality, to accentuate Wolsey's size. We had to have a window because he looks out of it, a table because he is sitting at it, a candle because he needs light. Nothing else was necessary, emphasizing just claustrophobia and the power of the political cleric. The natural temptation was to make a palatial set for a cardinal, but we resisted that. Orson Welles, by the way, caught on at once. He looked at the set, instantly disappeared and came back with red rims around his eyes! That whole effect, to me, was what is meant by designing. In *The Leopard* (1963), Visconti showed his genius in putting a particular dance scene into a ballroom which was *too small*. A beautiful salon with an enormous polished floor would have been all wrong – in that particular instance – but how many directors, and through them their designers, would have resisted the temptation, particularly in a period piece? The danger is always that a designer might fall in love with his own sets.

'Take another scene from *A Man for All Seasons*, when King Henry VIII arrives by river to visit More. What did we want the audience to feel about this well-known king? It was the present-day equivalent of a fine fellow out for the day in his Aston Martin. Construe that into the period. Those boats had to have a certain dash and style. We had to create an *image* of the boats to correspond to the Aston Martin, not to a Rolls Royce. In reality the Royal barges would have been much larger and grander than ours – and a designer could have had a field day building enormous and ornate vessels which would have filled the screen. We deliberately resisted this and ignored reality, making them smaller and moving with *élan*; the whole giving a sense of gaiety on a lovely English day.

'Then take Fagin in *Oliver!* (1968). Until I knew the colour of his coat, and until his make-up and whiskers were correctly worked out, I was uncertain about what should go behind him. Period architecture and period clothing can conflict on the eye and become disturbing. Which comes first? The clothing. Get the character right in his clothes before you move into the background. They should look like clothes, not costumes.

'Another vital factor to the designer is style. Before starting anything he must be intimately familiar with the overall style in which the film is to be made. This having been agreed with the director, he must never waver from it. In addition, it is important to know what his camera lenses can do for him. When talking over a set with the draughtsman, I discuss it in relation to the lenses which might be used and the movements of the camera. The cameraman or the director may disagree, but you, yourself, must be certain of the image you want and this can only be achieved by what the camera eventually photographs with a particular lens. These lenses range from the wide angle through the 500 mm. with its extreme telescopic effects and the choice of lens can go a long way towards giving the emotion required.

'I prefer locations when possible. There is something wrong about building things that are already there. However, one must accept that it is a choice generally governed by economics. The important thing to remember is that no exterior set should be built arbitrarily. There must always be a reason for its existing where it does. The country house in *Dr Zhivago* (1966, directed by David Lean) was built beside a clump of trees in an open plain. This took away any feeling that it was placed there simply because it was convenient for the people who were making the film. The trees anchored the house into the wide landscape, which in turn gave scale to the house, and the people who came to it.'

Though it might seem that colour would enlarge the scope of the production designer, Box states that in most cases he would use black-and-white if he had the choice.

'In the great majority of films you are telling a dramatic story in pictures about people, and adding colour is merely bringing in an unnecessary extra complication. Often you find yourself actually fighting colour to stop it imposing itself on the story unnecessarily and destroying concentration. The biggest battle the designer has to face is competing with the emulsion of the film, which if uncontrolled will give you a glossy "chocolate box" rendering. Another point to be remembered is that in colour it is difficult to get anything to look really ugly. It puts a false gloss on everything. And when all these worries are over, of course, there is the possibility of your work being altered in the processing at the laboratories. When I was working on *Our Man in Havana* (1959, directed by Carol Reed) we had the choice between making it in Spain in colour, or in Havana in black and white – a balance of economics. Without hesitation, I voted for Havana and black and white.

'To give one more illustration of what I think designing for films means: the mirage scene in *Lawrence of Arabia* (1962, directed by David Lean). We had worked out the mirage effect, using a 400 mm. lens and a cutting device. To bring a man from a mirage to the foreground would have taken something like twenty minutes, so we cut the film in such a way that the cuts on the mirage grew shorter and shorter and those on the reaction from Lawrence and his guide, longer and longer. We had picked the location on a vast salt flat in Jordan and studied the times of the day when we would get the ideal light conditions. We had to add a well, which was a script requirement. Lawrence had been brought by his guide to this landmark, and they were resting. The edges of these blinding salt flats ran into black basalt which was like black pebbles loosely flung on to the white surface before the basalt took over, and the whole floor of the desert became a shiny black. It was not possible to site the well among this basalt and still achieve the ideal mirage of the lone bedouin approaching the well, so we painted the basalt on to the salt flat in fingers so that the eye was attracted to the white shimmering horizon. The desert is also interlaced with camel tracks; these had been worn on to the surface by the passing camels over hundreds of years. Almost by instinct, at the last moment I took a painter with me and we painted a

long white line, representing such a camel track, across the
expanse and into the distance towards the point where the mir-
aged rider would appear. When we'd finished this job I thought
no more about it, but immediately after the scene was shot,
Peter O'Toole told me: "You don't know how much that line
did for me! The effect was extraordinarily eerie, and very com-
pelling." That white line had had a sort of hypnotic effect on the
actor. Designing isn't just sets!'

In designing sets, purely practical points have to be borne in
mind, as Ted Marshall points out:

'However inspired you feel as to the appearance of a particular room or building, walls must be movable so that the
camera can make its own exits and entrances, and invisible
joints must be arranged so as to disguise the fact that the room
comes to pieces. Blending location with studio shots is another
problem. Front doors and halls can be particularly difficult in
this respect. You will often have a "real" front door, shot in a
London street, leading to a studio hallway. Most front doors
have one or two steps leading up to them. If, as generally happens, there is a scene photographed from inside the hall, looking
out of the front door as a visitor approaches, these steps must
be apparent. This means that you have either to build the entire
hall set, with possibly stairs and other rooms, on a rostrum, or
you have to lead down into the hall by an equivalent number
of steps. The first is quite likely to result in creaks, groans and
wobblings, the second looks unnatural.

'There is no need, fortunately, to be too rigid in all details. In
The Key (1958), we had a cupboard in a hall, at the bottom of a
flight of stairs. In one scene it opened on a hinge to the right, in
the next the hinge was on the left. The director, Carol Reed,
changed it over because the second time a right-hand hinge
didn't work in with the shot. No one noticed!

'Location choosing may take a very long time: we spent six
months on *The Charge of the Light Brigade*. It's essential
where possible to have three or four alternatives in mind, and
particular matters such as transport have to be remembered.

It's no use choosing a marvellous setting in the middle of a bog.'

Elliot Scott, who was supervising art director at the former MGM Elstree Studios, describes his methods when working as designer:

'First of all I consult the producer as to the scale of production he has in mind. Then the director. Any film should be the director's work, aided by everyone else, and it is most important to establish very early how he proposes to shoot. For instance, a director may use very narrow angles for some intimate effect. This means that only the area on which he is concentrating will be established, and the remainder will be out of focus – the opposite of, say, the deep focus work on *Citizen Kane*. All this has to be taken into consideration. The classic method of starting each new sequence with a long-shot, proceeding to a modern medium, and then close-shots, is seldom used nowadays, and a director will often begin on a close-up of, say, an ashtray. There might be no long-shot at all, so an effect of luxury or poverty, or even a whole dramatic atmosphere, may have to be established through a series of details such as these. And they must be planted where they will be seen. Then, working from the script, I produce simple ground plans to scale for each set or location. These are estimated by the construction department for inclusion in the main film budget. The production manager will have drawn up an ideal order of shooting based on considerations such as availability of cast, and I try to make this work from our end by checking all sets against available stages, trying to allow adequate building time, and so on. When this doesn't work, and it frequently doesn't, then it's back to the drawing-board, or some form of horse-trading with the production office to arrive at something mutually agreeable. This can be a huge dovetailing job, but stage space is expensive and often in short supply.

'Now I can start on the final (one hopes) designs, which of course have been forming in my mind all along. The drawing-office produces scale drawings (several hundred on an average film) and the set decorator his lists of all props needed. We discuss colour schemes with the dress designer. The drawings are issued to the construction department, who then re-check their estimates. Sometimes we make continuity sketches to cover difficult areas of action, or special effects, or to tie up interiors with locations – and then we start to build the sets.

'An example among many of practical designing occurred in *The Haunting* (1963, directed by Robert Wise). Here we had a house which was in itself an evil entity, attacking the unwelcome people staying in it. To give this impression of gloom and menace was, of course, fairly straightforward. But a number of scenes took place in a library where the threat was more explicit. The room contained a circular staircase which, seemingly deliberately, disintegrated gradually while somebody was standing high up on it. This meant that the staircase had to be designed so that it looked solid, could move and shake, could break, but at the same time was strong enough to support not only the person on it, but also the camera, which was attached to it and ran up and down on a special device.

'Not only the requirements of the director and cameraman must be considered, but also those of the sound department. Until a few years ago, for a dialogue scene taking place in a ballroom we would use paper floors to prevent the noise of dancing feet from smothering the voices; then came stiletto heels, and the end of that device! The problem is not so acute now, with the improvement in recording techniques, but it is an indication of the variety of questions to be answered. But above all, the art director must try to add something to the film – something of his own contriving to enrich the final result. Otherwise there's no point in using sets.'

7. The Costume Designer

The costume designer is responsible for clothing every man, woman, child – and sometimes animal – in the film. There is, at present, no training course for the designing of film costumiers. The approach differs from that of the theatre designer, because the film designer has to decide how materials will photograph, what will happen to the various colours in the camera, and afterwards during processing, which fabric will stand up to the scrutiny of close-ups, particularly on the wide screen, even what sort of noise it will make as the wearer moves around. Most costume designers, like Julie Harris who provides a description of her job below, are freelancers.

'On each film my first job is to read the script and make a breakdown of the costumes needed for the principals. I generally start with the ladies, but if the male star is more important I attend to him first, because everything else will revolve around him. I work very closely with the production designer, discussing the overall colour scheme of each scene, and with the producer and director on the kind and the cost of the clothes required. Very early on I have to consider what happens to each outfit – does it go in the water, does it have anything spilt on it? A constant nightmare in this respect is how many takes the director will shoot – how many copies of a dress will be needed if it is to be spoilt each time. I also have to work in with the hairdressers to a certain extent, especially if hats are involved: this requires tact, as hairdressers don't welcome very much interference. Eventually, however, after a good deal of adjustment (particularly in a modern story, because everyone has his or her own idea of what is smart), the designs are agreed.

'The next task is choosing the materials. I have a very useful personal assistant who helps in this, but there's always a time when you have to look for yourself. This means many hours going around the shops and wholesalers. You need masses of patterns, and some retailers are not keen to give you very many – or they may simply be sold out. A lot of materials, even wool, come from France, where they have a much fuller range of colours, and this involves delay in delivery. Once the materials and patterns are finally selected, I farm the work out to costumiers and dressmakers. This applies to the costumes for the stars and leading players. For smaller part and crowd artists, clothes will be hired or bought, or they may even wear their own. Few studios have much stock these days, but one hopes to find military or hospital uniforms, old coats, overalls, etc. Smart clothes nearly always have to be made, and may go back to the costumiers afterwards. I quite often see on television costumes which I have used already in a film. In all this work I initiate and delegate: I tell the assistant director or the wardrobe supervisor what is needed – the fittings for a period picture may amount to three or four hundred for a single sequence. But I am solely responsible, even if it is only for saying to whoever is instructing the crowd, "Tell them please to come in summer dresses," or "I don't want anyone to wear blue," or "As much black and white as possible." The advent of colour has, of course, made the business of selection very much more complicated. It is also necessary to think of what a material will sound like. In the early days of talkies costumiers had a terrible time with stuff like taffeta. Nowadays things are easier, but neck-microphones, concealed inside an actors clothing, can be a damned nuisance.

'Jewellery, shoes, underclothes – often difficult – are my responsibility, and so is armour (generally fibre-glass, or, if it's chain mail, weighted knitted wool which is often not heavy enough to look realistic), together with sword belts and gun holsters. The sword itself is a property and is the property master's responsibility. The dividing line between properties and costumes is often vague. Umbrellas and watches are properties, handbags are costume. So, rather oddly, is camouflage. It's a matter of liaison between the two departments. Checking the correct details of uniform and armour can entail a vast amount of research. In big spectacular scenes much of the background stuff is fake – soldiers with made-up rollpacks and equipment, painted webbing on a painted uniform. The old theatrical rule that there must be something wrong with a military or police uniform no longer holds good, but there very often is!

'In the musical version of *Goodbye, Mr Chips* (1969, directed by Herbert Ross) I had to provide four periods of school uniforms, 1903, 1924, 1942 and 1968. The last two were simple. For the wartime coupon years we could get away with "no uniform", and for 1968, the boys of Sherborne School (where the film was shot) wore their own uniforms, but with "our" ties and hats.

'My work goes on right through shooting, and I generally feel the need to be present at the studio every day. I may be the only person who knows exactly how a dress should be put on, and of course there is always the chance that somebody won't like something and we shall have to make a change in a hurry. Once it is all over, the hired and stock costumes are returned, the bought or made ones can generally be purchased by the artists. In fact this does not often happen. By the end of the film they are usually fed up with their clothes. Sometimes a star will be made a present of her wardrobe. Ursula Andress, for instance, was given all the costumes she wore in *Casino Royale,* including some wonderful fur coats. Costuming can account for a considerable share of a film's total budget. Those for *Casino Royale* amounted to $30,000 and for *Goodbye, Mr Chips,* $50,000. In the latter, Petula Clark had forty changes (they grew in number as the filming proceeded), and two sequences each demanded dresses for 200 women. All told, 2,000 costumes were made for *Chips*.

'I don't think films set fashion trends nowadays as they used to. In the old days a Joan Crawford picture, for instance, would have a strong influence. It may continue to a greater extent in America, where there is a big commercial trade and coast-to-coast advertising. *Darling* (1965, directed by John Schlesinger) created the "Darling look", and of course there was the thirties explosion afer *Bonnie and Clyde* (1967, directed by Arthur Penn). One recent blessing has been the easing of censorship. We don't have to worry so much now about such things as cleavage and navels. And tights have been a godsend!'

8. Special Effects

The special effects department is concerned with the *physical* side of the particular action sequence involved. The *optical* work, matting, double printing, comes under the heading of special effects, though the laboratory side is usually referred to as process work. In an earthquake scene, for instance, the toppling buildings and gaping earth-fissures might be arranged by special effects, perhaps also involving a number of stunt performers: the spectacle of fleeing, stricken crowds will be superimposed later by the laboratories. The two very often work closely together, double printing or matte work being combined with models. In *One Million Years B.C.*, actual small volcanoes in the Canary Islands were photographed in eruption, and afterwards these were tied up optically with full-size studio sets where the ground opened and people fell into abysses – on to cardboard boxes covered with mattresses. Until about the mid thirties there were no special effects departments as they are constituted nowadays. Certain people had an aptitude for doing certain things – creating effective controlled explosions, perhaps, or manipulating model trains – and gradually tended to specialize.

Cliff Richardson, a freelance special effects director, regarded as the 'explosives expert', and George Blackwell, in charge of special effects at ABP studios, Elstree, have provided me with information on some of the problems involved and the methods employed to solve them.

In a battle, a lot of balancing is required between small arms, mortars, and big explosions. All explosives are pre-set, and markers are placed facing away from the camera so that the horsemen and foot soldiers can see them and pass either side. This is often tricky, as smoke and dust may obscure the markers. As a rule the explosions are set off automatically but in very difficult instances they can be fired manually from a switchboard, the operator watching for suitable (and safe) moments. The explosive charge will be placed in a steel mortar buried in the ground, the direction of the force being controlled by the shape of the mortar. In *Duffy* (1968, directed by Robert Parrish) Richardson was presented with a fishing vessel 'souped up' with special engines, which had to blow up and sink in forty-five seconds. The scene was to be shot from a helicopter: no one could be in the boat and no connecting wires could be used. Richardson fixed time clocks on the side of the boat, allowing the staff three minutes to get away before the circuits went into action. Radio control was then used to blow up the ship.

For the famous bombing raid in *The Dam Busters* (1953, directed by Michael Anderson), George Blackwell had a model dam, about fifteen to twenty feet across, erected in a studio set of lake and countryside about one hundred feet square. The dam was originally to be blown up by model aeroplanes, but it was found physically impossible to create a miniature column of water which would stay in the air long enough to look convincing, even with the aid of a high-speed camera. Instead the surface of the water was disturbed by submerged air jets and a film of an actual full-scale explosion was superimposed.

Buildings to be blown up are generally cut away beforehand into the required segments and loosely fastened together, but in Robert Aldrich's *The Dirty Dozen* (1966), on which Cliff Richardson worked, the particular set had to stand up to six weeks of night shooting beforehand. This meant that it had to be substantially built, and blown up without any preparation. In *The*

Battle of Britain (1969, directed by Guy Hamilton) 160 charges were placed in the brick piers to blow up a real aeroplane hangar. Cases like these demand expert knowledge of where to place the charges for maximum safety. 'Often,' says Richardson, 'I'll be asked by the director how close someone could be asked to stand without being in danger. I'll point out the nearest spot, and the director will immediately want to put the unfortunate actor nearer still, to liven things up a bit.'

The effect of a stream of bullets striking along a road or bouncing off rocks is achieved by pre-setting small explosive charges and firing them off in rapid succession (very tiny ones are sometimes even planted in an actor's clothing); alternatively they may be represented by gelatine capsules, such as are used medicinally, filled with french chalk and fired from a self-loading compressed-air gun. This method requires great skill from the special effects department, and great trust from the artist! Knife throwing: the character at the receiving end wears a steel plate with a wood or cork block attached to it. From the block a length of piano wire extends to a 'knife catapult' which keeps the wire taut as the man moves around. On the knife are a couple of eye-hooks or a small tube through which the wire is threaded and kept in place by a pin and a button. At the desired moment the button is pressed and the pin withdrawn, the knife flies down the wire and – all being well – sticks in the wood. The editor generally cuts to a shot of the knife actually penetrating. This method may be used with arrows, or the 'flip-up' arrow may be used: a short length of the foot of the arrow is fastened beforehand to the victim and held flat against him by a spring which is released on cue. Flaming arrows are bound with a plastic igniter cord, a form of fuse which, once burning, will not be blown out by the rush of air. Arrows in bulk are usually fired in batches of fifty or so from a compressed-air tube with cotton waste as a washer to propel them. Flung spears are treated similarly but in individual tubes.

Fire: 'real' flames are apt to look transparent, so colour is added to enhance the effect. Bottled gas is generally used, with a 'conflagration plant', which is a series of jets through which is pumped petrol and either diesel oil or paraffin, dependent on the colour of flame and amount of smoke required. Controlled by a tap and a high capacity pump, flames can be made to leap forty feet. If a wall is to go up, petroleum jelly will be coated on it and ignited by remote-control gas jets out of camera range. The result looks terrifying, but is under complete control. On the word 'cut' the gas is turned off and everything returns to normal. For the famous sea-on-fire sequence in *From Russia With Love* (1963, directed by Terence Young) the sea was prepared for about 500 yards with cellophane bags floating just under the surface, each containing five gallons of petrol. These were ignited on cue and exploded, the bags being blown out of the water and covering the surface. Everyone concerned wore asbestos suits, and the diesel-engined boats were similarly protected. Even so, Young says, two of the boats caught fire. 'In all such effects,' says George Blackwell, 'my first concern is the safety of the artists, my second the safety of the camera. There's no time to consider anyone else – they have to look after themselves. One's aim is to achieve the maximum effect first go-off so that re-takes are unnecessary. It's all a matter of calculated risk, and extremely convincing disasters can be worked within reasonable limits. While working on the story of the *Amethyst* (in which we used the actual ship), my fire effects, under complete control, were so convincing that the Royal Navy VIPs who were watching were horrified. They thought I'd done what the Chinese couldn't do – sunk the damned thing.'

Glass to be shattered in a free-for-all used to be made of sugar. Fox's Glacier Mints were the most popular makers, and the cast and technicians were often to be seen walking among the wreckage eating the splintered windows. Nowadays a very brittle plastic moulded in the plasterer's shop is used.

The special effects department also controls, to some extent, the weather. Rain can be piped from ten-foot tanks below the studio floor to three-inch mains above the stages, from which flexible pipes lead down. Blackwell has perfected a rain nozzle in the form of a half-sphere with holes of varying sizes. The sphere can be made to revolve, jets of water are trained on it, striking veins inside and bouncing off, something in the manner of a very elaborate garden spray. It has the advantage of completely silent operation. Snow has always been rather a problem; everything from feathers to bleached cornflakes, soapflakes and plastic shavings has been used, without any great measure of success. Some years ago Richardson designed a nozzle for spraying a modified firefoam, and this idea has recently been resurrected using a polyurethane foam. Real snow can be made and, though not a very practicable proposition, is sometimes used in close-ups. A foam bath is rapidly frozen with dry ice, and the result has to be shovelled out as quickly as possible, before it melts. For fog and mist a non-toxic oil is vaporized and spread from pressurized cylinders. Dry ice, once popular, is still sometimes used, but has the disadvantage that it is not persistent. It swirls too much and leaves gaps. A recent innovation is liquid nitrogen with oil vapour, the nitrogen serving to cool the vapour. Sal ammoniac was much in use before the war and, as Blackwell states, 'nearly killed everybody'. The most common practice is to use a fog filter in the camera in conjunction with artificial mist in the set. Wind and waves (in studio tanks) come under the jurisdiction of electricians and plumbers, but are of course combined into the general effect. Both are obtained by the use of giant machines.

Cobwebs are flung around by a conical cup with a lid which is held away from the rim by a spring. The latter can be adjusted to make an extremely narrow opening. The cup is filled with rubber solution thinned out by a solvent and linked to an electric drill with a fan. The mixture is sprayed out, and clings to everything and everybody within reach.

The alluring and apparently everlasting mountain of foam which fills the actress's bath to the brim (and served, in less permissive days, to keep her covered with sufficient modesty to avoid a censor's cut) is kept to the required height and opacity by the prosaic means of reinforcements pumped through a pipe on the floor of the bath.

Disasters such as train crashes and car pile-ups generally involve model work, but are often just what they appear to be. Minor accidents, for instance break-away wheels, are frequently pre-set and worked by the actor or a stunt man. Cliff

Richardson devised a method whereby a chariot wheel would detach itself during a chase, either by remote control or by the pulling of a lever by the rider, and it is likely that in future more and more effects of this kind will be set off by radio. Richardson has, in fact, recently made considerable use of radio-controlled model planes in *The Battle of Britain*. 'For the big train crash in *Lawrence of Arabia*,' he says, 'the last coach was loaded with sand to provide the impetus for it to crush those in front of it; the whole train was then filled with dummies and rifles protruding from the windows. It was a vast undertaking. Three-quarters of a mile of track was specially laid, and the locomotives and rolling stock had to be transported by road to the shooting site.'

Sometimes the real thing can look more like a model than the model itself. 'In *The Italian Job*,' says Douglas Slocombe, 'there is a death-defying stunt where cars are seen leaping from one roof-top to another. Even our own colleagues found it hard to believe that this was not in fact model work. Such instances really need a human being visible to indicate the relationship with actuality.' High-speed cameras are commonly used with models to slow down the movement. A derailed toy train will fall in a couple of seconds, a real train would take much longer. A cameraman will work out the difference, multiplying scale by time in a purely arithmetical computation. Another essential is to cut all model work as short as possible – never to show the full length of an effect. 'However good it is,' Slocombe says, 'cut it by half.'

The doyen of model specialists is Ray Harryhausen, whose unique contribution to special effects is the conjunction of fantastic models – particularly prehistoric monsters – and real people, a process he has named 'dynamation'.

'Dynamation,' he says, 'is a very intimate combination of live and model work. My prehistoric animals are always seen with real people. I never merely cut away from one to the other. This is half the value of a fantasy film, and you get much more realism of action – in the fights between men and beasts in *One*

Million Years B.C., for example. I call my process dynamation to distinguish it from animation, which is mostly used to denote flat drawings. The latter have often been combined successfully with real people, but the three-dimensional effect of models is obviously more satisfactory. In order to create credibility, a model may, indeed, be much more rewarding to work with than a living organism. The one real lizard we used in *One Million Years B.C.* gave a hopelessly lifeless performance, it wouldn't even blink one eye.'

Harryhausen's aim is to portray fantasy with conviction rather than to mystify by trickery. From the earliest stage, he translates a story from verbal to graphic images.

'As soon as a script is completed I make dozens of sketches, large and small, of the sequences in which my models will appear. Sometimes the producer and I will even start with my large sketches, and write a script around them. The final articulate models are made with my own hands, using a rubber compound over a jointed framework. In the case of prehistoric animals I follow exactly the details of their appearance which I obtain from various museums. The backgrounds and real people are photographed first, and the animals inserted afterwards against a blue backing or back projection. Then the whole thing is rephotographed. High-speed cameras are used sometimes to give the impression of slow falls, and lighting has to be very carefully matched to blend in the live and the model portions. Colour is much more interesting than black-and-white, but it adds enormously to the problems. All this can take a very long time indeed, and it may take up to a year to complete the animation after the rest of the film has been shot. Nine months was spent on the model work in *One Million Years B.C.* In *Jason and the Argonauts* (1963, directed by Don Chaffey) there is a scene where the hero battles with seven skeletons. All seven had to be synchronized separately with the live hero. He was photographed first, acting as if he was a sevenfold shadow boxer. Everyone on the set had to *imagine* what was happening. Then the separate pieces were assembled together. This short sequence, lasting only a very few minutes, took nearly five months to complete. In *Jason* an added problem was the presence of water, which always increases the difficulties of model work.

'Comparatively little dynamation processing takes place in the laboratory. After the live film is shot, most of the putting together is done photographically in the camera. Even such scenes as that in *One Million Years B.C.*, where the prehistoric bird grabs the girl and flies off with her, was done directly in the camera.'

Harryhausen considers that the term 'special effects' is probably confusing to an audience. 'It means so many things that in the end it means nothing specific. There is, for example, what is known as "floor effects", which includes fire, bullet-holes, gunfire, and so on. Then there is the "matte painting", where a section of the live set is painted on a sheet of glass. There is rear projection, for the interiors of moving automobiles and explosions in battle scenes. All come under the general heading of special effects. Dynamation is a specific form of special effect.'

He detests the idea of making fantasy films with tongue in cheek. 'This is fatal. If the audience is to believe in what it sees on the screen, then the creators must believe even more strongly. Every medium of expression has its own forte. Because of its greater flexibility the film, more than any other art form, was made to portray fantasy. The fantastic film can be as real and relevant as any other category. The problem of *One Million Years B.C.* is the problem of today – how can a more advanced tribe bring progress to a less advanced one? And as for reality – Willis O'Brien injected into a pile of rubber and metal joints far more sympathy and depth of character than was to be found in the real people on the screen when he created his masterpiece – *King Kong*.'

9. The Continuity Girl

The commonly held idea that the job of a continuity girl is to note down that an actor is wearing a red tie with blue spots when he enters a room, so that he will not be shown wearing a blue one with red spots when he leaves it, is only a fraction of the truth. Angela Allen, who among her other assignments worked for ten years with John Huston, says:

'One of my first tasks is to time the script. This can only be an estimate, of course, but after a while you get fairly accurate at working out how long a dialogue scene or an action sequence will last. I attend every rehearsal, noting down all the general changes. During shooting I also record the camera lens used in each scene, the filters, the camera's distance from the object it is photographing, on which word of dialogue it moves and in what direction, whether it pans or zooms, and in which direction the characters are looking throughout the scene. In a shot of cars or moving people it is very important to note the direction, because if something or someone is seen moving from left to right in one shot, it is confusing if at the start of the next shot they are moving from right to left. An actor's expression must be matched up as nearly as possible (from a medium- to a close-shot, for instance) but this is extremely difficult because sometimes six or more takes will be printed and no one knows which piece of which the director will eventually choose. There's neither time nor money to match every detail in every take, so I often have to compromise. Fortunately, style is much freer nowadays, which allows a certain flexibility.

'It is important for a continuity girl whenever possible to be an aid to the director, even risking having her head snapped off by suggesting, "I think you need a close-up here, or a long-shot there." She must be ready to point out loopholes in the script, places where the dialogue doesn't make sense, or where a scene is running too long, and she must ensure that enough covering material is available so that the editor can remove something if necessary.

'During the shooting day she has to type on to what is called a continuity sheet a detailed description of every scene which is made. On this sheet goes the information about the cameras, the printed, held and bad takes, all the dialogue and the moves in the dialogue. It shows exactly where the shot starts and on what word it ends. Sometimes one manages to do the typing between shots, but when the director is shooting exteriors, or very fast, all the typing has to be taken home and the day can be very long, sometimes ending around midnight. It is definitely not a glamorous job.

'The trickiest problems occur when a character gets his clothes messed up – either as part of the story or by accident. A scene in itself is generally shot in continuity, but the individual sequences are not. I remember one occasion when a man had to be seen getting out of a boat and running up a beach. It was the last day of shooting: the scene had to be shot during a couple of minutes of twilight: the man had only one jacket. The part where he ran up the beach after leaving the boat had already been filmed, and in it he was perfectly dry. Then the scene of him getting out of the boat was shot. He fell into the water and was practically drowned.'

10. The Editor

By many directors, editing – which can be described very simply as the assembling and joining of selected pieces of film – is regarded as the creative peak of the entire film-making process, the preliminary shooting being largely a matter of collecting together the necessary materials to be assembled into a coherent whole.

In Russia, as is well known, the importance of editing was recognized and exploited from the very early days of silent films, but elsewhere, and particularly in Hollywood, the completed picture would be removed totally from the control of the director and handed over for this essential treatment to a studio employee, who might be as much a hack as many of the routine scriptwriters in their little boxes. The director might never set eyes on his work again until after its release – and then might have difficulty in recognizing it. It was said in extenuation that cutting followed such a regular and conventional pattern that anyone by simply following indications on a script could do the job successfully: nevertheless it is true to say that embittered directors have expressed themselves (and still express themselves on occasion) more forcefully over this 'distortion' of their intentions than over any other form of alleged interference with their privileges. Nowadays the director who does not follow closely the editing of his own picture is an extreme rarity.

This is not to belittle the contribution of the editor himself, who can bring an objectivity and freshness of vision to a work with which its creator has been very long and closely involved, and can frequently make artistic as well as practical suggestions of great value. Of all parts of film-making, editing is probably the best stepping-stone to directing, and many directors have graduated to their present position from the cutting-room. The editor sees almost every move of the game from beginning to end, and can learn practically all there is to learn about making films, with the important exception of how to direct actors.

The potential influence of editing on the finished product can scarcely be exaggerated. It can quicken the action by the removal of alternate frames, or slow it down by the insertion of additional ones; it can ensure a smooth progression or jerk an audience from scene to scene with shock cuts; it can totally alter the meaning and significance of a sequence, or even the entire film, by revealing one aspect before another; it can, as Eisenstein demonstrated in an everlastingly quoted instance, bring stone lions to life. It can ruin a potentially good film, and can to some extent rescue a poor one – but this is not so easy.

The tools used in editing are a synchronizer, a moviola, a joiner or splicer, and a china-clay pencil. The synchronizer is an assembly of parallel spools in pairs. On one of these is wound the picture reel and on the others (one or more) the sound tracks. The picture reel passes over an illuminated frame between the spools, and the sound tracks over magnetic heads – enabling the operator to match up exactly the sound and visual tracks at the moment of the clapper-boy's actions as he brings down the wooden arm on to his numbered board at the beginning of each take. The moviola, through which the reels are run after synchronization, is a viewing machine, worked by foot pedals to leave the operator's hands free. He sees the film at a little less than postcard size, with an adequate sound reproduction, and can reverse, stop or slow it at will. The splicer nowadays replaces the somewhat awkward glue-acid method which was formerly used to cement the cut portions of film together, and which often resulted in a loss of frames on either side. The splicer uses very fine scotch tape, and is quick and simple to manipulate. The tape is sufficiently thin to avoid causing any noticeable loss of quality in the frames it covers as they flash past at the speed of twenty-four frames a second.

The editor receives each day the material which has been shot the day before and processed during the night. His first step is to number and log each shot, each take of each scene. Alongside every foot of film is a different number and letter; these are also on the original negative and logged in the laboratory. Everything is also entered up and assembled by 'slate numbers' (from the slate on which the clapper-boy chalks the number of the take), in accordance with the continuity sheets. These references enable every foot and each shot of the film to be easily traced both on the cutting-room shelves (where the reels are stored in numbered boxes) and in the laboratories. He next assembles the takes which the director has selected after seeing the rushes, and matches them up with the corresponding sound track on the synchronizer. This sound track, it should be noted, is the original 'live' one recorded during the actual shooting. It will be filled with extraneous and unwanted noises – such as passing aeroplanes, traffic, children shouting – if made on location, and is rarely retained for the master print, though many directors prefer to preserve live dialogue if it is at all possible. In other cases it merely stands in as a guide for the editor. (The sound and visual tracks are never physically joined together ('married') until the fine print stage is reached.) The editor then feeds both tracks through the moviola, marking with his china-clay pencil the unwanted portions such as the clapper-boy's performance and any other pre- or post-shot fragments, cuts them away, and tapes the joins. With these preliminaries concluded, the real work of editing begins.

Kevin Brownlow describes his job as an editor:

'The director generally chooses each take, and the first assistant editor (as a rule there are two assistants, one wholly concerned with logging and filing) lines them up in order – that is, assuming the director has any ideas on the subject. On an action sequence he frequently does not, unless he has himself been an editor. You then assemble the shots as "unroughly" as possible. There are no rules – no theories – just a little voice inside you which says "yes" or "no". You *feel* when it is right. Logic is death to editing – you become literary, whereas all that matters is what is right cinematically. You take a sequence to the theatre, run it, take it back, worry it into another shape, run it again, take it back, tear it apart, start over once more . . .

'The continuity sheets are more important as a guide than the script is. You only refer to the script if it's relevant to the sequence. This is because quite often the director will not shoot according to his script, whereas the continuity sheets, drawn up afterwards, are a record of what he *has* shot. The most important instinct for an editor to possess is a sense of timing – a sense of the correct rhythm for each individual scene and for the overall picture, and of how these should contrast or correlate. The opening and closing moments of a shot are vital because you need to give the impression that life has been going on before you cut into a scene, and is to continue when you cut from it. There is only one perfect frame on which to cut – three out either way can make all the difference, even allowing that each one lasts only one twenty-fourth of a second.

'Having selected and put together the day's shooting, the editor hangs the pieces of film on a rack over a large bin ready to be spliced together finally in a rough cut. The rest is filed away: nothing will be destroyed, even after the master print is completed, in case it may one day be of use. It is also the editor's job to choose stock shots (battle scenes, a stock-exchange panic, establishing shots of cities or famous buildings) from the studio library. The advent of colour, though it does not much affect the actual cutting, may present problems when looking out stock shots, because of the increased care necessary in matching the print qualities with those of the new film.'

Another description is given by Tony Gibbs:

'Editing is putting into dramatic from the celluloid the director has filmed – generally consisting of several takes for each scene, from various angles, close-, medium- and long-shot. Once he has his material (i.e., the director's choice of takes) the editor should be left alone to assemble it, noting (1) the tempo of each separate scene; (2) the emphasis which must be given to any particular character; (3) the overall rhythm of the film. One reason I like working with Richard Lester or Tony Richardson is that they prefer you to go away and "surprise" them with an assembly, rather than to give you definite instructions. After all, it's possible for an editor to bring out of a film something the director had not even realized was there – another viewpoint. And if the editor's viewpoint proves disastrous, there is always the director's own concept to return to. The running of the rough cut often shows the unexpected: what looked marvellous on the printed page may look very different on the screen. A brilliant scriptwriter provides two pages of excellent dialogue, and then the actor conveys it all with one glance, and renders every word redundant.

'I find the most difficult problems are posed by a sequence such as the hunt in *Tom Jones* (1963, directed by Tony Richardson). One has virtually no guidance from the script (which might merely say, "There follows a hunt"), nor any dialogue or obviously "follow-on" action to give a lead. Somehow out of this mass of assorted material I had to show, under all the surface *joie de vivre* and excitement, how fundamentally cruel a foxhunt is. In *Petulia* (1967, directed by Richard Lester) the difficulty was to find a suitable style. For all its highly original treatment, and despite all the flashbacks and flash forwards, it was deliberately edited in a flat, unobtrusive fashion: there were no pyrotechnics, no subliminal effects. It was this cool approach, I think, which paradoxically prevented the film from appearing cold.

'Devices such as fades and dissolves come within the province of the editor. He decides which effect is needed, marks it on the print, and the laboratories carry it out. The old traditional fade from one scene to the next is hardly ever used nowadays. As in music and painting, there are periods when the artistic rules are consolidated and developed, and periods when they are broken.

At present in the cinema the rules are being broken – brilliantly, for example, in *Tom Jones*. However, free style can be over-done and become an undisciplined hash. This is apt to occur with directors or producers (or editors!) who are too inex-perienced and brash to wish to bother about knowing the rules they are going to break.

'Discarded film is kept, because you never know when you may need it. United Artists, the distributors of *Tom Jones*, never expected to receive a seal of approval from the Catholic Office. One day they rang from America to say that if we would make two small cuts the seal would in fact be granted. In order to remove the two portions satisfactorily we needed to replace them with other material. Because we had stored the discarded strips away, I was able to take what I wanted to America and substitute it for the offending shots.

'The process of fine-cutting is, as the word indicates, a pro-cess of refinement – an adjustment of tempo and emphasis. You might have to alter the whole aspect of a character in the story – possibly even bringing the actor back to the studio and giving him new words. One newly recorded line can sometimes re-place an entire unsatisfactory scene which had hitherto inter-rupted the flow of the film. You might have to slow things down by double-cutting silent close-ups from one performer to another, putting in pauses which were not there. You might even have to steal a piece where a player is sitting waiting for the director to call "action".

'In *The Loneliness of the Long Distance Runner* (1963, di-rected by Tony Richardson), the opening scene with the school governor looked good in its original form on the page, and even when it was first put together on film. But finally it didn't seem to work. So, long after everything had been shot and cleared away in the studio, we turned the whole thing upside down – starting with the end of the scene, progressing to the middle, and finishing with what had been the beginning. It was a change from a failure to a successful scene, all done by juggling around with pieces of celluloid. That's what editing is about, and what makes it so exciting.'

David Gladwell describes his work as editor on Lindsay Anderson's *If* . . . (1968):[1]

'For the start of shooting, a unit of eighty-five people, plus actors, set off for Cheltenham, the first location. At the same time, I moved into the cutting-room in Bayswater which was to be home for several months. A booking of three weeks for final sound track dubbing had already been made at a sound studio for a date five months ahead – a deadline I wondered if it was possible to meet. With me in the cutting-room I had two assistants.

'When the rushes (both picture and sound) come into the cutting-room, one of the first jobs to be done is to number everything. That is the boring task of the second assistant. Before that, however, he has synchronized the rolls of sound with the rolls of picture. Each roll needs to be done scene by scene throughout the roll. As this will be material shot the previous day and processed overnight, the urgency arises because the director and the cameraman are obviously very anxious to see the results – the current day's shooting may depend on it. In the case of *If* . . ., with the unit away in the provinces, I viewed the rushes, sometimes with one of the London-bound producers, and then made telephone contact with the unit. The film, without sound, was then transported to Cheltenham for the unit to view at the local Odeon late at night.

'We dealt with an average of 2,000 feet of film each day. This is twenty minutes' running time of rushes. The style of shooting is highly controlled in this film. . . . Each camera set-up is very precise, but without being self conscious, and all camera movements are carefully rehearsed and executed – the opposite of a "cinema-verité" style. One direct result of this was that one take of a scene was often almost identical to the last. . . . Although at the time of shooting it was the director who requested retakes, when it came to editing, he was the first to admit that there had often been no necessity for them. The supercharged atmosphere

1. Extracts from an article in *Screen* (January/February 1969), the journal of the Society for Education in Film and Television, edited by Kevin Gough-Yates.

on the floor when shooting contrasts with the relatively relaxed situation in the cutting-room and one's responses vary accordingly.

'The rushes having been synchronized and viewed, the panic over for another day, clerical work sets in. This is mainly the domain of the first assistant. Every foot of film must be recorded in a log. The slate and take numbers will have been photographed on the front of each scene shot. These can be listed together with the film edge-numbers in each case. With continuity sheets and log properly organized, there is no reason why any foot of the 100,000 feet shot should not be located within seconds of being required. No reason, it is true, but we do have some anxious moments at times.

'In a typical documentary situation, even when [a] production has started off with a detailed script, circumstances during shooting will have compromised the original intentions to some degree. The technique of editing at such times often consists of sticking bits of film together until something begins to happen. It can, I suppose, be termed a skill, based upon experience, to recognize the fact that something is beginning to happen and also the direction in which it is going. Very important in editing, as perhaps in most arts, is an appreciation of the value of accidents and chance. One is continually having to make a decision: whether what has just been created by joining two bits of film together is valuable and is to be developed, or is of no value and is to be disposed of in the formation of another attempt. The first try at editing any sequence is usually very unsuccessful, and so one works on it in the manner described. On the other hand, there are times when shooting has gone very much according to plan and on these occasions one starts cutting in a more logical way: an assembly is made of a generous amount of the footage shot, put together in script order but without being specific about cutting-points – that is, allowing plenty of overlaps and repetitions of actions within the scene.

'By the time the main part of shooting of If . . . was complete and the director was due to move into the cutting-room, most sequences had been assembled in script order. So obsessed with perfection is Lindsay Anderson that . . . no cut satisfied him until all the possible alternative arrangements of shots or alternative frames on which to cut had been fully considered. The accuracy of cutting throughout was usually to one twenty-fourth of a second – that is to a single frame. In the case of static, held long-shots, this precision might fall to one-twelfth of a second; we would discuss whether to take off six, four, or two frames – never, for some reason, the odd numbers. There were times when a decision was difficult to make between the excising of, say, six or eight frames. Occasionally, at such times, I would risk my reputation and our relationship on seven frames – and, as likely as not, it would be acceptable. Perhaps differences of one twenty-fourth of a second are not detectable; but differences of a twelfth of a second certainly are – and this always amazes me.'

11. The Composer

There has never really been such a thing as a silent picture. Almost from their first public showing movies were accompanied by a pianist, or a phonograph, or even on occasion by actors or singers standing beside the screen and trying to synchronize their voices to the action. Volumes of 'mood music' were profitably published, neatly labelled to enhance scenes of deep emotion, tragedy, comedy, knock-about, danger, flirtation, horror, despair, and of course, love. The 'mighty Wurlitzer' soon added its organ voices, ranging from *vox humana* to side-drum and cymbal, and by the time the true sound film arrived, the musical accompaniment to the silent film had reached – in the larger cinemas – a standard which is difficult to realize today, with perhaps a thirty-piece orchestra and a battery of sound effects. Though the desk lights and the conductor's baton were sometimes distracting, there is no doubt that the arrival of the large band, replacing the solitary matinée pianist, tuning up and bursting into full blast – even though it occurred at a fixed hour regardless of what was happening on the screen – gave the whole proceedings a splendid fillip.

Though there were notable instances of specially composed scores, music was generally selected from existing works, either chosen by the musical director of the cinema or recommended by the production company. With the arrival of sound and the possibility of a permanent and more specific musical score, the film composer came into his own. In the following pages, three composers talk about their methods of work and the problems to be solved in the preparation and recording of a score.

John Barry

'The composer's most important responsibility is to tell the producer and director what he thinks is right. For instance, the decision as to which parts of the film should be accompanied by music should be his. The main problem is that of form – how to write in a given time a piece of music which has an intrinsic structure and form away from the picture, which is a dramatic entity in itself. This is not very often possible, because in general the music has to be subservient to the picture. Occasionally one is offered a happy exception. In *Deadfall* (1968, directed by Bryan Forbes) there is a sequence where a robbery is carried out in a house while the occupants are listening to a first performance of a guitar concerto at a hall in the neighbourhood. In this instance I composed a complete work which was recorded first, and the film was shot and edited to my timing. At some points the relaxed moments in the concerto were deliberately matched to contrastingly tense shots in the sequence, so that instead of merely underlining the action the music slightly characterized it. I found this very satisfying, but it is an unusual opportunity. Another "different" instance was *Four in the Morning*, in which my music was integrated with the sound effects.

'The ideal function of film music, to my mind, is instanced in *The Lion in Winter* (1968, directed by Anthony Harvey) where there is scarcely a bar in the whole score which *directly* heightens the dramatic action. The choral score in Latin, for example, brings another dimension to the picture. It has a voice of its own, and is a complete counterpoint to the action.

'If a film is badly designed, the composer will be used to reinforce it, to try to conceal the weak joins, so to speak, and this results in musical cliché such as the surging up-swell of

sound to emphasize rising emotions. Sometimes, of course, their
use is fully justified – in the James Bond series, for instance,
where the accompaniment is really a parody of conventional
film music.

'Once it is decided what the music should and should not do
in a picture, the editor gives the composer a timing sheet containing all the action and dialogue broken down to one-third of
a second. He sets to work from this guide, in conjunction with a
moviola. In my early days I found this minutely exact timing a
frustration, but it's really just a matter of technique, and now it
doesn't worry me in the least. I find it impossible to work from
the script alone. It's absolutely essential to see the footage, because so much may be altered during shooting. I read the script
of *The Whisperers* (1966, directed by Bryan Forbes), for
example, but when I saw Edith Evans on the screen she was
playing the part quite differently in terms both of performance
and of sympathy. I do nothing at all until I see the rough cuts. I
then start work on the thematic material, completing my score
against the fine cut.

'At a recording session the composer works from a score
heavily marked with timings. The orchestra is rehearsed, then
the film is projected on a screen which is visible to the conductor, but not to the players. A second rehearsal follows, with
the picture and the second-counter, or flasher, beside it, after
which the conductor starts going for takes. He needs three eyes
– one on the orchestra, one on the score, one on the flasher. He
also listens to the dialogue on earphones. It's not an easy procedure, and many composers find it impossible to cope with. I
always attend dubbing sessions, because the musical emphasis
can be radically changed at this stage by the sound editors. And
then, after all the trouble you take, everything can be ruined by
careless projection!

'Writing music for films can be very demanding, but even in
the limitations of the cinema I find a lot of freedom. After all,
it's no more restricting than the discipline of any other form of
composition – the difference is merely that it is a discipline
imposed from outside rather than from within yourself. You
have to learn to register your effect in perhaps thirty seconds. It
can certainly teach you a great deal about composition, and is a

perfectly valid art form, which has interested many of the greatest twentieth-century composers.'

Richard Rodney Bennett

'The film composer used to be looked on as a sort of first-aid man, called in to help over a bad patch, a car chase which wasn't exciting enough or something which wasn't very stimulating creatively. Nowadays he is usually brought in earlier and his music is regarded as an integral part of the film, particularly by certain directors, for example Joseph Losey and John Schlesinger. His music should comment, not underline; it should be interesting but not intrusive, weaving its own colour into the film without hanging on to its crucial moments. This is what I tried to achieve in *Secret Ceremony* (1969, directed by Joseph Losey). It's a very strange film, for which I made a very strange score. Earlier I followed the general tendency to play safe – now I find it much more interesting to do a score like *Secret Ceremony* where I can really go my own way. Often a score can make its point by apparently completely contradicting the atmosphere of the scene it accompanies, perhaps by hinting at some sinister significance in a situation which is not yet apparent. A good example of this occurred some years ago in *The Bad Seed* (1956, directed by Mervyn LeRoy), where an innocent scene of a little girl in a garden being seen off to school by her mother was underplayed with incongruously menacing music, anticipating the revelation that she was a child murderess. I don't think that even definitely anachronistic music matters if you can create a style suitable to the film. A composer could use a beat group or a sophisticated jazz score in a picture set in the eighteenth century as long as it was done with taste and imagination, and was coherent.

'The number of players for any movie is limited by the budget, but it can be varied within these bounds. I find that the more films I do the smaller are the instrumental groups I prefer. There is a general tendency nowadays to move away from the enormous symphony orchestras of Hollywood in the thirties and forties. For *Secret Ceremony* I used only six players.

'I don't like to read the script first. I prefer to see the whole film when it is completed – not even the rushes, but the actual fine cut. I view it first right through, then reel by reel, and gradually ideas come. I start off as a passive onlooker until I become stimulated by what I am watching. I don't even necessarily have to work with the director. There have been occasions when he has actually left the country to start another picture before I began to write the music. Of course, if you are involved with someone with a real knowledge and love of music, someone like John Schlesinger with whom you can really get *en rapport*, it can be very helpful to work closely with him.

'I enjoy the practical side of film composition. I find the limitations of time, etc., very stimulating. I first work out a skeleton score with the exact number of bars at my disposal, then gradually develop it into its full form. I always do my own orchestration – it's half the pleasure of film music, because you can sometimes be more experimental than in "serious" music, always provided the result bears out the point in the picture. I never conduct, because I think the composer is more useful in the recording room, but my score has every indication, every point of synchronization marked on it, and provided it is played at the correct speed everything should fall into place.

'In animated films the usual process is reversed, the music being composed first and the animation matched to it. A score I completed for an animated picture by Richard Williams was based on a series of drawings he showed me before I began work: he then, as it were, filled the gaps between them. Documentary films I find much less satisfying, partly because they are generally loaded with a heavy commentary.

'Film composition can be mentally exhausting, but even if I were rolling in money I should still want to do it, simply because I love it so much. It is, of course, pleasanter when you reach a stage where you can exercise a certain amount of selection regarding the type of films you do, and I have found it advisable to limit myself to, say, one or two pictures a year. After all, the average amount of music in each film is about 40 minutes – two modern symphonies or one big romantic one. I emphatically disagree with those people who say that writing music for films must have a bad influence on a composer's "serious" work. I learnt more from composing film music than from three years' study at the Royal Academy. It was an immediate practical experience, one had to be infinitely adaptable and technically skilful.'

Dimitri Tiomkin

'I never composed music for silent pictures, but when I was a student at St Petersburg I used to earn a little money by playing the piano at one of the local cinemas. I remember accompanying a film of the great French comedian Max Linder, and at one point I was so overcome that I laughed out loud. This was such a success with the audience that the manager asked me to keep it in – an early example of providing both music and sound effects. In those days most of the people providing music for motion pictures were complete ignoramuses – second-grade musicians operating in New York – never seeing the pictures – just writing general descriptive pieces which were filed in a library. When sound was invented, these people were replaced by composers with real musical knowledge, people who wrote for the sake of the film, not merely to please themselves. This change, together with improvements in the recording system, led to the real revolution of background film music, and the whole business began to get properly organized. The music of a motion picture had real box-office value.

'Now, once again things have changed. Basically the reason is a financial one. The industry is going through a big economic revolution. Companies like to save money, so, while still increasing enormously the salaries of the big stars they go to the other extreme in those departments where they choose to cut down. A big symphony orchestra, eighty or ninety players, all on union rates, is very expensive, so, seeing that in television they had small combinations, the producers thought: "Why should we engage all these people to play in films?" Sometimes of course, small groups are very successful. For *High Noon* I had very few players; in *Champion* (1949, directed by Mark Robson) I used only brass and woodwind. But many pictures need the full sound of a symphony orchestra, and very often it is not possible to give it to them. The period when music itself was considered very important to a film is already yesterday. Today producers like to have just sound. But music *is* important – it is a very vital factor in giving rhythm to a motion picture, in heightening climaxes, in colouring the whole text. It is a challenge to the composer similar to that of a ballet score. Film is a new combined form of artistic expression, and is still only experimenting with sound as an extra element of this combination. I do not myself believe that electronic music will replace ordinary music in the cinema, though admittedly it can be very interesting as an additional source of added sound.

'I have never written film music with concert performance in mind. The two forms are entirely different. The film composer's duty must always be to enhance the picture – not necessarily situation by situation but as a complete work. Motion picture music is music for motion pictures. When people buy the music on records afterwards, it's primarily to remind them of the film, not because of their interest in the music itself. I found this marriage of music to picture a great problem when I started. Now, after 160 films, it can still sometimes be restricting. The variations of the theme song in *High Noon*, for instance, were not easy to work out – but it is all really a collaboration between the director, the producer and the composer. Sometimes, like with Frank Capra in *Lost Horizon* (1937) I manage to get a chance to do a lot of things I want to do. Ideally, of course, the music should be written before the picture. Years ago, Irving Thalberg wanted Arnold Schoenberg to compose music for a film and asked how he would like to work. "I write the music first," replied Schoenberg, "then you make your film to fit my music." For background music this doesn't often happen; but occasionally, with very famous music, like the Strauss waltzes I arranged for *The Great Waltz* (1937, directed by Julien Duvivier), the camera follows the music. *The Great Waltz*, by the way, was also the first time multiple channels were used, producing stereophonic music.

'The most exhausting part of film composing, however, is not the restriction of form, but the time limit. The picture is finished; you ask, "When do you want the music?"; they reply,

"Yesterday!" I know Mozart composed the overture to *The Marriage of Figaro* in one night, and Rossini was pretty quick with *William Tell*, but today a film composer is expected to write in three weeks miles of music – and to a stop watch.

'Before I start work I see the film and make suggestions about cuts – which are generally accepted – I'm not an easy man! But a knowledge of form is the first sign in a musician that he knows his business. I always conduct, and I attend the dubbing sessions when permitted – which is *not* always. It is very important that a composer should do so, because his work can be ruined by sound editors: ask Stravinsky about *Fantasia*, or Aaron Copland. You have to be a real fighter!

'One reason I have turned to production is to ensure that I can do what I want to do. In my film life of Tchaikovsky the star is the music. The interest of the man Tchaikovsky is that he wrote this music – why he wrote it, the state of mind that caused him to write it. When he is composing the Fourth Symphony, it is the Fourth Symphony that matters. At the end of the picture, when Tchaikovsky is dying and we have the Sixth Symphony, I am dropping all the illustrative element. After a film of three hours – three hours of creative and psychological study – I think we have the right to show music to the audience *au naturel*. I should like to have the screen in darkness, but that might be a little dangerous, so – with no fancy montage, no camera tricks – we shall just see the orchestra, and listen.'

Jack Clayton's admiration for Georges Delerue's score for *Jules et Jim* made him determined to obtain him for his own film *The Pumpkin Eater*.

'We could hardly speak to each other. I know three words of French and he knew one of English, but we achieved an understanding which did not require words. What I did in *The Pumpkin Eater* was to get a whole series of compositions from gramophone records and piece them together in rough synchronization to the film, just to show him my feeling about the various moods, and where the music should go. We played the film first with the dialogue, then with my record selection, after which Delerue went home and composed his own score. This worked admirably. In any case, music can't be conveyed, unless you are a musician. A composer says to you, "What kind of thing do you think it should be?" and it's almost impossible to describe satisfactorily. With *Our Mother's House* I showed him the rushes quite early on, and from watching these he was able to grasp the sort of thing that we needed, and to create the score he finally brought to the film.'

12. Sound

Microphone (Boom operator)
|
Console (Sound mixer)
|
Sound camera (Recordist)
|
Sound track (Dubbing editors)
|
Married print
|
Cinema projector
|
Loudspeakers

The above is a skeleton chart of the progress of *live* sound (dialogue and effects) from the studio floor to the screen. In practice live sound effects – i.e., those recorded during actual shooting – are scarcely ever used nowadays, particularly on location, for the obvious reason that a microphone will pick up unwanted as well as wanted sounds. The same difficulty often applies to the dialogue also, but this is retained whenever possible, as it generally has an immediacy and spontaneity which may be difficult to regain later in a recording studio. A. W. Lumkin, recording director at Associated British Productions, Elstree Studios, describes the various processes involved:

'In the case of a feature film starting on location, the sound engineers will take out lightweight, transistorized equipment and try to record the dialogue at the same time as they shoot the picture – concentrating just on the voices and certain minor sounds which go with them, such as movements of the actors or the rustle of their clothes. The main problem is the exclusion of extraneous noise. This is much more difficult in the case of a period film: a background of motor traffic or an occasional passing plane may pass as background to a conversation between two people in a present-day park, but not in an eighteenth-century garden. Small radio microphones concealed in the actors' clothing are sometimes used, but these are subject to interference from other wavebands. Another device is a neck-microphone with a cable to the mixer – a cumbersome device, worrying for the actor, and in any case only usable when the wearer is stationary.[1] Much more convenient nowadays are "rifle mikes", ultra-directional microphones which can be pointed towards the required source and are able to pick up dialogue under adverse conditions that would be impossible with conventional microphones.

'When the unit returns to the studio much the same procedure is followed, only the dialogue and immediate sounds being recorded for possible use. Here the sound mixer is captain of the crew, seated at a small transportable console on the perimeter of the set. The studio microphone is attached to a large, silent and infinitely adjustable boom. The boom operator feeds the sound to the mixer, who makes his preliminary selection of volume ratios, in turn feeding it back to the sound recordist. In addition, the boom operator must have considerable knowledge of camera angles and set-ups, as he has to place his microphones as best he can for sound recording without at the same time causing interference to the cameraman. The mixer always attempts to record as much usable dialogue as he can. Ultra-directional microphones are sometimes used in the studio as well as on location, but you cannot beat a good mike on a boom with a good operator and a good mixer.

'There is a tendency nowadays to record all dialogue during shooting on quarter-inch magnetic tape in the first instance, rather than on the 35 mm. magnetic film which was the practice until recently. The usable material will then be transferred from the tape to 35 mm. magnetic film, sent to the cutting-room, matched up with the picture by the editors, and eventually joined up in story sequence.

1. Sandy Dennis, on location in *Up the Down Staircase:* 'I sometimes wore a battery mike strapped to my leg, or else one which was hung inside my clothes with a wire running right down my body and out through my shoe, while somebody hid behind me keeping it free!'

'So far we have dealt only with the acceptable live dialogue and incidental sounds. The next step is post-synchronization,[2] the replacing of unsatisfactory lines by the actors concerned after shooting is finished. This is done in a specially-equipped studio by a procedure known as "looping". The actor stands before a screen on which will be projected the scene to be post-synchronized. A film recorder with a special erasing head is used. The film on this machine is made up in a loop of about 60 feet, and the strip of picture film is similarly looped. A section of the original dialogue is also recorded on a loop to give a feeling of action. On cue, the sound and picture loops are started off in synchronization. The actor watches himself on the screen, and listens on headphones to what has already been spoken. On the picture there is a leader and a wipe – a pencilled red line which moves across the screen. Taking his cue from this, the actor re-speaks the lines to match his lip movements. He can continue to do this for as long as is necessary, and each time the section comes round his voice will be erased and re-recorded. As a rule the looping session is presided over by the director, with the sound mixer responsible for quality and the editor for synchronization. When they think everything is satis-factory they call "check!", and the record head is switched from record to replay so that the lines can be listened to in conjunction with the picture. Sometimes an actor may have to go round the loop twenty times before the welcome "check!" is heard. Once passed, this post-synchronized dialogue will be laid in synchronization with the corresponding picture to make up 1,000-foot rolls of film.

'Sound effects may be divided broadly into two sections: (1) those obtained from pre-recorded sound libraries, generally the "bigger noises" such as battle sequences, thunderstorms, pistol shots and ricochets, earthquakes, trains, surging seas, mobs,

2. The terms 'post-synchronizing' and 'dubbing' are often used indis-criminately. The simplest way to avoid confusion would be to retain 'post-synchronization' for speech which really *is* synchronized, for example, an actor re-speaking his own lines, and to reserve 'dubbing' for occasions when it is slapped on regardless, as in foreign-language dubbing. The same differentiation could apply to sound effects. When they are intended to synchronize, use the word. Otherwise – dub.

traffic; and (2) those recorded in the studio specially for the film in question – body and clothing movements, chinking of jug against glass, closing and opening doors, tapping on windows. A very important item in this category concerns footsteps: many studios have stretches of cobblestones, paving, sand, gravel, etc., permanently laid down, and there are specialists in reproducing the different types of steps. All these effects are recorded on separate tracks, as are music, speech, and sometimes a commentary, which will be made independently.

'It is not unusual for a feature film to finish up with 6 tracks of dialogue, 5 tracks of music, and 24 tracks of effects, making a total of 35 separate strips of recorded magnetic film. All this material will have to be manipulated, merged and mixed together to give one composite sound track. Sometimes a pre-mix will be made first, by putting together, say, half a dozen tracks so as to lessen the number which will have to be handled during the main sessions. The whole operation, which may take several weeks, is carried out through a mixing desk (or dubbing console). This large recording machine, at which will be seated three or more technicians, may have anything up to forty or more inputs through which the separate tracks are fed from banks of film playbacks, all run together in synchronization by an electric generator. In the Associated British studios at Elstree, all direct sound, proceeding from shooting films on perhaps seven stages simultaneously, is piped through to one central recording area, with obvious advantages of economy and convenience. From this central storehouse the relevant tracks are now sent out as described above. A projector is linked to the film banks, and through this the picture film is run, together with the footage indicator. The technicians at the console, working from cue-sheets and cues on the screen, watch the film and mix together all the different sounds, raising one level, lowering another, cutting short a third, until the picture is completed. If the film is in stereo another technician, seated at a small console below the mixing desk, receives the sound from the desk and channels it into the appropriate speakers. Then the composite track, still on magnetic film, is transferred to optical film, and the laboratory "marries" sight and sound (the sound

also now being visible in the form of waving lines) on to one
final master.

'Though optical sound tracks are still in general use, mainly
because few cinemas other than the largest or most recently
built are equipped to play magnetic film, the latter is far preferable. Optical film has a frequency range so limited in comparison that it is like playing an old 78 r.p.m. gramophone
record against a modern long-player. This difference is particularly noticeable in the case of sharp sounds such as bells,
cymbals or shots, but even with speech you can hear the
difference in overtones. I am always pushing to get magnetic
sound into every cinema, but you have to be sure that their
equipment is properly set up to play it adequately – being so
much improved in quality, it is also much more critical.

'In spite of all the care taken, when a film is shown in your
local cinema it will sometimes appear "out of synch". There are
four possible reasons for this: (1) it could be that the post-
synchronized dialogue has been badly matched by an inexpert
dubbing editor; (2) the tracks may not have been very well laid
at the time of joining; (3) it could be due to incorrect synchronization at the laboratory; (4) it could be due to faulty lacing by
the cinema projectionist. The sound head of a projector is
placed twenty frames ahead of the vision head, and this has to
be allowed for in the printing operation. In lacing up the film
there is also some latitude, and the twenty-frame separation
must be maintained. If this is not done, either movement or
sound will appear to happen first. But even if the film is correctly laced, synchronization will only be perfect to someone
seated fifty feet from the screen, because of the varying speeds
of light and sound. He is not, however, very likely to notice the
difference! (On television, incidentally, the telecine operator
must lace up at nineteen frames instead of twenty, because few
people do their viewing in fifty-foot rooms.)'

13. The Distributor

Distribution is the marketing of the film as a finished product. The distributor's job is to distribute (i.e., rent) the picture to the cinema, and later, if possible, to television, and his responsibility is to show as great a profit as possible. The distributing company is usually allied closely to a major producing company – it may also be allied to a chain of cinemas. The process of distribution, however, remains much the same, whether or not it is allied to other interests. The completed prints are delivered by the production company to the distributor, who has agreed to rent them for a certain number of years, the copyright of the film remaining in the hands of the production company. The distributor handles all the post-production publicity and exploitation of the film, generally advancing the cost of these and recouping the amount from the producer's share of the box-office receipts. The distributor himself also receives a share of the receipts and has therefore a direct monetary interest in raising these as high as possible.[1]

Having received the film, the distributor (in Britain) endeavours to secure a West End of London booking. This is regarded

---

1. David Gordon points out 'the little-known fact that in practice, because of their generous distribution fees, distributors hardly ever make a loss on a film' (*The Economist*, 8 March 1969).

mainly as a shop window, any receipts from such a run being frequently swallowed up by publicity costs. Following the London showing may come (1) the pre-release – that is, bookings ahead of the London release; (2) the London release; (3) the provinces. The pre-release cinemas are certain selected houses in the London district (but outside the recognized West End) and in the large provincial cities. The London release pattern includes most of the major cinemas on the outskirts of London and in the major suburbs. There are, of course, frequent and often sudden variations in the above sequence: an unexpectedly long run in London itself, an equally unexpected failure which has to be pulled out, sometimes a picture which has been scheduled for a limited run in the West End but which has done so well that it is brought back again later. The whole pattern of distribution is keyed to maximizing audiences, firstly in the best theatres, and later in the less important houses.

The British distributing companies run sales forces which extend across the country, calling on independent cinemas in their particular areas (the big circuits have their main offices in London), carrying literature and trade reports, as in the marketing of any other type of goods. The distributing companies are also responsible for seeing that prints of the films are made available for cinemas in good time for their play-dates. They arrange various private showings, such as the press show and the trade show. The latter is compulsory by law, in order to give every exhibitor the chance of seeing a film before he books it. 'Blind booking', where an exhibitor is expected to screen a film which has not been trade shown, is illegal. The press show is voluntary, a facility for the convenience of the critics, sometimes held in a small private theatre by restricted invitation, sometimes a full-scale screening in a large cinema. Not every film is press shown, and a producer or director will sometimes withhold permission in a special case. Tony Richardson's *The Charge of the Light Brigade* (1968) was a recent example.

Arnold Barber, Managing Director of Warner Pathé Distributors, says:

'The difference between marketing films and marketing

other products is that in our case the product has to be completely paid for in advance. If you are selling an article such as a fountain pen you can make a few thousand, and then if it is unsuccessful you can forget about it. With a film, if the final cost is ten million dollars, the whole lot has to be paid out before we can make a start.

'If anybody finds that a film has been cut after its first screening, they always use the word "distributor!" We are not *empowered* to cut films (which we generally see before the censor does). We may consider that some part of it could be offensive or might be improved by a little trimming here or there, but we never cut a film without the producer's cooperation. It has happened that a film has been shortened after it has been shown in the West End; we ourselves don't like this, but it may be thrust on us by the producer. Can you blame a man who has a commodity to sell, finds something a little bit wrong, and adjusts it before it goes to a wider public?'

14. The Censor

Every film intended for commercial showing in Great Britain must pass before the British Board of Film Censors. This is an unofficial body, established in 1912 by the film industry itself, but retaining its independence and freedom from pressure owing to the method by which it is financed. A fee, based on length, is charged for each individual film, and payments are never made by the industry as a whole.

The British Board of Film Censors consists of a president, a secretary, and five examiners, three men and two women. There are no explicit rules governing their decisions on the films they view: judgement is based on experience and on what the Board considers the limits. The Board classifies films for public showing in three categories:

U: suitable for universal exhibition, with no restrictions on the admission of children over five (or seven if in London), which is the minimum age.

A: suitable for anyone over sixteen, or under sixteen if accompanied by an adult.

X: suitable only for those over sixteen.[1]

1. Since this book went to press a new category system has been drawn up, which came into operation on 1 July 1970:
U: passed for general exhibition

With the exception of newsreels, everything which is shown on the commercial screen comes under the scrutiny of the BBFC, including advertisements, cartoons, and trailers.

Apart from the BBFC, censorship can be, and sometimes is, exercised in Britain by other bodies, for example, the local authorities, who are empowered to refuse or withdraw licences in cases where cinema managements show films such authorities consider objectionable. This power was granted more or less accidentally by the 1909 Cinematograph Act, originally intended solely as a move to ensure adequate fire protection. It was to protect their own interests that the film-makers set up the BBFC, and to avoid the inevitable confusion caused by a multitude of concerns exercising independent censorship. As a general rule, local authorities now abide by the Board's decisions. There are, however, exceptions from time to time. The Greater London Council, for instance, have permitted public screenings of films refused a certificate of any category by the BBFC.

Under John Trevelyan, Secretary of the present BBFC, the Board pursues a policy of considerable elasticity to suit the climate of the moment. In November 1968 Mr Trevelyan gave an illustrated lecture on the work and intentions of the Board under the auspices of Derek Hill's New Cinema Club, at which were shown extracts of films which had either caused difficulty in the past or were then still refused certification. A few months later Mr Trevelyan stated: 'Already, if I were to give that lecture again, my selection of films and subjects would differ considerably from those I showed on that occasion.'

Consideration is always given to whether a particular scene

A: passed for general exhibition, but parents/guardians are advised that the film contains material they might prefer children under fourteen years not to see.

AA: passed as suitable only for exhibition to persons of fourteen years and over.

X: passed as suitable only for exhibition to adults. When a programme includes an X film no persons under eighteen years can be admitted.

The certificates will be seen on the screen in colour: yellow for U, green for A, blue for AA and red for X.

The raising of the X category age will enable the Board to pass certain films which would otherwise (or have hitherto) been refused certification.

has a real purpose in the film as a whole or is put in for sensationalism. The chief stumbling blocks to obtaining a certificate are, of course, violence and sex – in that order – and in particular any combination of the two. Mr Trevelyan has commented:

'Violence is not only a question of degree, but also a question of reality or unreality. In the old conventional Western there was plenty of "bang – you're dead" action, but no one died realistically, and no one got hurt or was seen in pain. When the market for these films decreased they were made with increasing realism, which took them from the U to the A category; now we frequently have brutal and sadistic Westerns which can only be accepted in the X category.

'There are certain themes which we do not consider suitable for the entertainment of children; particularly such themes as corruption, sadism, drugs, abortion, homosexuality and sex perversion. A passing reference, or implication, may be acceptable, but anything explicit, whether visual or verbal, is unlikely to be.'

Nudity in itself has not been frowned upon for some years – witness the numerous coy presentations of shrub-protected torsos in the exquisite boredom of nature camp movies. The famous 'pubic hair controversy' over the Swedish *Hugs and Kisses* in 1968 was raised, says Trevelyan, quite deliberately to test public reaction, and in fact paved the way for the passing untouched of the longer scene in Lindsay Anderson's *If . . .* (1969) where the housemaster's wife wanders naked through the deserted school corridors. He has since told the company distributing the former film that they could reinstate the brief cut if they wished to do so.

Horror films, rather surprisingly, do not often come under the guillotine, unless they combine sex with violence. The most vulnerable sequences are probably those dealing with witchcraft, where the Board has been accused of excessive sensitivity. A complete sequence was removed from Roger Corman's *Masque of the Red Death*; Mario Bava's *Black Sunday* (or *Re-*

venge of the Vampire) took several years to achieve release at all; and fifteen seconds were cut from Roman Polanski's *Rosemary's Baby* after the press and private screenings.

A film which has been refused a certificate in any category always stands a chance of being granted one at a later date. *Black Sunday* is a case in point: another one is the Yugoslavian film *The Switchboard Operator*, directed by Dusan Makavejev. The Board has sometimes been surprised by unexpected reactions. Jack Clayton's *Room at the Top* was regarded in 1958 as a 'breakthrough film' in England, on account of the so-called frankness of its dialogue in one or two scenes, and Trevelyan was congratulated on his courage in passing it. 'I couldn't understand this at the time, and looking back now I can understand it still less!' On occasion he has even been attacked in the press for *not* sufficiently censoring a film – for example the Boulting Brothers' thriller *Twisted Nerve* (1968).

The situation in America is somewhat different and more complex. In the 1920s, censorship was practically non-existent. The industry then began to come under pressure – because of the nature of certain films, and because of a succession of scandals such as the Arbuckle trials and the murder of William Desmond Taylor – particularly from the Catholic Church and the women's organizations. This led to the setting up by the Motion Picture Association of America of the Hays office, an organization much more closely tied in with the industry than the BBFC, but with the same basic aim of protection. All companies agreed to make their films in accordance with a document called the Production Code. This was drawn up largely under Catholic influence, and was very rigid. It inevitably became pretty liberally interpreted as time went on, and in 1965 a new President of the Association, Jack Valenti, made the liberalization official. At about the same time the Supreme Court ruled the censorship of films before screening to be illegal. These two factors combined to swing the moral pendulum quite far in the opposite direction. Frankly pornographic films moved out from hiding, into the more respectable quarters of the towns and cities, and the industry began once again to come under criticism. In November 1968, therefore, they brought in a classification system composed of three categories (G, M and R) to which they are prepared to give Code Seals, and in addition an X category which is given to films submitted and not approved, and also to films not submitted.

Jack Valenti discusses this classification system:

'This is how we describe our four rating categories:

G: for general audience (suitable for all ages, though not necessarily a "children's movie").

M: for mature young people, with parental discretion advised (find out more about this film, Mr and Mrs Parent, but you make the decision about going).

R: for restricted, an adult film from which children under sixteen are barred unless accompanied by parent or adult guardian.

X: patently an adult film, with children under sixteen barred.

'In an almost unchanging pattern since the programme began on 1 November 1968, approximately 75 per cent of the features have qualified for the two top categories, while Rs have run around 20–23 per cent and Xs to 6 per cent. Our surveys show that the rating system is being well supported in the industry and well received by the public. Already, since the programme began there have been far fewer legislative proposals in states and cities to impose classification on films by law. We oppose all forms of statutory censorship. We do not, however, contest obscenity proposals not aimed solely at movies, but which in general provide that what may be proscribed as harmful to minors may not be interdicted as obscene for adults. This legal approach gives added impetus and meaning to the industry's voluntary rating programme, which is concerned with children.'

There is, however, as John Trevelyan points out, an important distinction between this system and the British one. In the United States it is on an entirely voluntary basis as regards the exhibitor. If he chooses to admit children to any film, nobody can prevent him. In Great Britain the chances are that if a cinema manager flouted the BBFC certificate he would be deprived of his licence by the local authorities, and herein lies the Board's legal power. In America certification is a protection for the industry, but its enforcement depends on the cooperation of those most likely to lose money by it. In the case of foreign films, such as those from West Germany, Sweden, Italy and other countries which may produce very explicit sexual scenes, once they pass the US customs (admittedly a formidable barrier) there is nothing to stop them being shown unless the police take action. In addition there is an agreement whereby such films need not put in for a Seal (the official approval of the Production Code); they are then, as stated above, automatically given an X rating, and are permitted to circulate throughout America in this category.

In theory, the Production Code lessens the chances of external censorship and at the same time curbs the exuberance of the sensationalist film-maker. These sources of external censorship are more numerous and complicated than in England. By far the most influential is the National Catholic Office for Motion Pictures – formerly the Legion of Decency and retitled in 1965. The Catholic Office classifies films not only in regard to suitability for children but also for adults.

Another important source is known as the *Green Sheet*, published and distributed by the MPAA. This is a monthly review of films, graded according to age suitability and briefly discussed. It is compiled by the Film Board of National Organizations, which includes various women's societies, the American Jewish Committee, the Protestant Motion Picture Council and other bodies. The Roman Catholic Church is not represented.

In both Great Britain and America scenes will sometimes be shot in different versions for screening in countries with varying degrees of censorial severity. Japan appears to be considered capable of assimilating the strongest diet of violence. And up to four or five years ago, according to the American director John Frankenheimer, 'we had to make cuts for England which were not necessary anywhere else'.

15. The Cinema

(Projectionist, Cinema Manager)

The number of cinemas in the United Kingdom in 1950 was 4,584. In 1967 the figure was 1,805, at the end of August 1968 it was 1,754, and in September 1970 it was 1,598. The weekly average of admissions in May 1970 was 3.3 millions, compared with 3.77 millions in May 1969. The following figures show the comparison with other countries, in 1967.

Decreases in the number of cinemas

	1950	1967
Italy	5,000	3,771 (commercial, all-year-round)

	1954	1967
USA [1]	14,716 (indoor)	9,953 (indoor)
	3,775 (drive-in)	3,670 (drive-in)

1. From recent figures given by Jack Valenti, the trend in the USA has been reversed. 'In 1968,' he says, 'there were 13,822 theatres in the US, divided among 10,129 indoor and 3,693 drive-in theatres. In the past six years new theatres have been constructed in the US at a rate of approximately 200 new theatres a year.'

Increases in the number of cinemas

	1950	1967
France	5,000 (approximately)	5,283
West Germany	3,900	4,714
Japan	2,575	4,296
Spain	3,900	7,395

Although the large super-cinema will always be necessary for the screening of the super-epic-spectacular, the trend at present is towards smaller houses. Older buildings are being converted into 'twins', and new complexes are being erected to contain two, three, or four mini-cinemas under the same roof. This activity is an encouraging counter-sign to the grim list of closures in the United Kingdom.

The hub of any cinema is, of course, the projection room, which may be anything from a palatial place, with electronic gadgets from ceiling to floor, to a glorified shed on the roof. Jack Isaac, chief projectionist of the Odeon Cinema, Marble Arch, describes his work:

'I have six assistants, working two or three on a shift. There are no chairs, as we are not allowed to sit down while working. Every reel is signed for. Every time a man laces up a reel he signs for it and then it is checked. He later signs a book to indicate that he has run the reel. Any complaints or peculiarities can be checked in the log book. Every picture is rehearsed first: this is essential as you might find you have been landed with one reel in French in the middle of an English version film – or two copies of reel 4 and none of reel 5. We are also responsible (in addition of course to quality of sound and vision) for the ventilation, heating and humidity of the auditorium. These can be affected by the size of the audience. We could alter the temperature on the spot, if only the public would ask us at the time, instead of writing in afterwards to complain that they were too hot and too cold, when it's too late to do anything about it.'[2]

2. In June 1969 a system of computerized cinema control, Cinetronic, was demonstrated at an ABC cinema. The system can provide a complete automatic programme of films – no projectionist need be present in the projection room. In the event of a breakdown, the computer switches everything off and rings an alarm for the projectionist to come and take over by hand. It can also work the curtains, the house lights, and can even turn spotlights on the salesgirls.

The most important attributes of a cinema manager, according to Roy Money, manager of the Odeon, Marble Arch, are
tact and a calm frame of mind. Apart from the business side of
running the cinema, the manager is the personal contact between all the work that has gone into the film, and the audience
for whom it exists. This is not always an unmitigated pleasure:
at one time he may be soothing an irate family who want their
money back because they "are bored by musicals and didn't
like the numbers anyway"; and at another time find himself in
hospital with six broken ribs after trying to stop a gang of
hooligans smashing seats and throwing things at the screen.
Apart from public hours, the building will frequently be in use
for extra screenings, press shows, trade shows, and business conferences, either in the morning or late at night when the audience has gone home to bed. It may be used by a production
company for showing rushes of a current project, if it is thought
advisable to see them on the big screen. 'Isadora was really put
together on the Odeon screen,' says Money. Under his authority,
the cinema manager may have a staff of anything from a dozen
to a hundred people – assistants, projectionists, box-office staff,
usherettes, salesgirls, cleaners, commissionaires, cloakroom
attendants, and others.

Bearing in mind that until it is actually unfolding on a screen
before the eyes of an audience a film is just so much celluloid in
cans, it can truthfully be said that every one of these people, as
well as the many we have already met in the course of this
book, are part of the making of a film.

Index